SELF-DEFENCE FOR EVERYDAY

Practical Safety for Women and Men

PADDY O'BRIEN lectured for over ten years at Southampton College of Art. She now teaches yoga and runs a personnel training consultancy. She is a black belt martial artist who has designed safety programmes for professional and open groups for many years. Paddy is the author of several books including *Managing Two Careers: how to survive as a working mother* (Sheldon 1989) and *Learning from Experience: a woman's guide to getting older without panic* (Sheldon 1990). Paddy O'Brien lives in Berkshire with her partner and five children.

Overcoming Common Problems Series

For a full list of titles please contact
Sheldon Press, Marylebone Road, London NW1 4DU

Beating the Blues
SUSAN TANNER AND JILLIAN BALL

Birth Over Thirty
SHEILA KITZINGER

Body Language
How to read others' thoughts by their gestures
ALLAN PEASE

Calm Down
How to cope with frustration and anger
DR PAUL HAUCK

Changing Course
How to take charge of your career
SUE DYSON AND STEPHEN HOARE

Comfort for Depression
JANET HORWOOD

Complete Public Speaker
GYLES BRANDRETH

Coping Successfully with Migraine
SUE DYSON

Coping Successfully with Your Child's Asthma
DR PAUL CARSON

Coping Successfully with Your Hyperactive Child
DR PAUL CARSON

Coping Successfully with Your Irritable Bowel
ROSEMARY NICOL

Coping Successfully with Your Second Child
FIONA MARSHALL

Coping with Anxiety and Depression
SHIRLEY TRICKETT

Coping with Blushing
DR ROBERT EDELMANN

Coping with Cot Death
SARAH MURPHY

Coping with Depression and Elation
DR PATRICK McKEON

Coping with Stress
DR GEORGIA WITKIN-LANOIL

Coping with Strokes
DR TOM SMITH

Coping with Suicide
DR DONALD SCOTT

Coping with Thrush
CAROLINE CLAYTON

Curing Arthritis – The Drug-Free Way
MARGARET HILLS

Curing Arthritis Diet Book
MARGARET HILLS

Curing Coughs, Colds and Flu – The Drug-Free Way
MARGARET HILLS

Curing Illness – The Drug-Free Way
MARGARET HILLS

Depression
DR PAUL HAUCK

Divorce and Separation
ANGELA WILLANS

Don't Blame Me!
How to stop blaming yourself and other people
TONY GOUGH

Everything You Need to Know about Adoption
MAGGIE JONES

Everything You Need to Know about Osteoporosis
ROSEMARY NICOL

Everything You Need to Know about Shingles
DR ROBERT YOUNGSON

Family First Aid and Emergency Handbook
DR ANDREW STANWAY

Feverfew
DR STEWART JOHNSON

Overcoming Common Problems Series

Fight Your Phobia and Win
DAVID LEWIS

Getting Along with People
DIANNE DOUBTFIRE

Getting Married
JOANNA MOORHEAD

Goodbye Backache
DR DAVID IMRIE WITH COLLEEN DIMSON

Heart Attacks – Prevent and Survive
DR TOM SMITH

Helping Children Cope with Divorce
ROSEMARY WELLS

Helping Children Cope with Grief
ROSEMARY WELLS

Helping Children Cope with Stress
URSULA MARKHAM

Hold Your Head Up High
DR PAUL HAUCK

How to be a Successful Secretary
SUE DYSON AND STEPHEN HOARE

How to Be Your Own Best Friend
DR PAUL HAUCK

How to Control your Drinking
DRS W. MILLER AND R. MUNOZ

How to Cope with Splitting Up
VERA PEIFFER

How to Cope with Stress
DR PETER TYRER

How to Cope with Tinnitus and Hearing Loss
DR ROBERT YOUNGSON

How to Cope with Your Child's Allergies
DR PAUL CARSON

How to Do What You Want to Do
DR PAUL HAUCK

How to Get Things Done
ALISON HARDINGHAM

How to Improve Your Confidence
DR KENNETH HAMBLY

How to Interview and Be Interviewed
MICHELE BROWN AND GYLES BRANDRETH

How to Love a Difficult Man
NANCY GOOD

How to Love and be Loved
DR PAUL HAUCK

How to Make Successful Decisions
ALISON HARDINGHAM

How to Move House Successfully
ANNE CHARLISH

How to Negotiate Successfully
PATRICK FORSYTH

How to Pass Your Driving Test
DONALD RIDLAND

How to Solve Your Problems
BRENDA ROGERS

How to Spot Your Child's Potential
CECILE DROUIN AND ALAIN DUBOS

How to Stand up for Yourself
DR PAUL HAUCK

How to Start a Conversation and Make Friends
DON GABOR

How to Stop Smoking
GEORGE TARGET

How to Stop Taking Tranquillisers
DR PETER TYRER

How to Stop Worrying
DR FRANK TALLIS

How to Study Successfully
MICHELE BROWN

How to Survive Your Teenagers
SHELIA DAINOW

How to Untangle Your Emotional Knots
DR WINDY DRYDEN AND JACK GORDON

Hysterectomy
SUZIE HAYMAN

The Incredible Sulk
DR WINDY DRYDEN

Overcoming Common Problems Series

The Irritable Bowel Diet Book
ROSEMARY NICOL

The Irritable Bowel Stress Book
ROSEMARY NICOL

Jealousy
DR PAUL HAUCK

Learning from Experience
A woman's guide to getting
older without panic
PATRICIA O'BRIEN

Learning to Live with Multiple Sclerosis
DR ROBERT POVEY, ROBIN DOWIE
AND GILLIAN PRETT

Living Alone – A Woman's Guide
LIZ McNEILL TAYLOR

Living Through Personal Crisis
ANN KAISER STEARNS

Living with Grief
DR TONY LAKE

Living with High Blood Pressure
DR TOM SMITH

Loneliness
DR TONY LAKE

Making Marriage Work
DR PAUL HAUCK

Making the Most of Loving
GILL COX AND SHEILA DAINOW

Making the Most of Yourself
GILL COX AND SHEILA DAINOW

Making Time Work for You
An inner guide to time management
MAREK GITLIN

Managing Two Careers
PATRICIA O'BRIEN

Meeting People is Fun
DR PHYLLIS SHAW

Menopause
RAEWYN MACKENZIE

The Nervous Person's Companion
DR KENNETH HAMBLY

Overcoming Fears and Phobias
DR TONY WHITEHEAD

Overcoming Shyness
A woman's guide
DIANNE DOUBTFIRE

Overcoming Stress
DR VERNON COLEMAN

Overcoming Tension
DR KENNETH HAMBLY

Overcoming Your Nerves
DR TONY LAKE

The Parkinson's Disease Handbook
DR RICHARD GODWIN-AUSTEN

Say When!
Everything a woman needs to know about
alcohol and drinking problems
ROSEMARY KENT

Slay Your Own Dragons
How women can overcome
self-sabotage in love and work
NANCY GOOD

Sleep Like a Dream – The Drug-Free Way
ROSEMARY NICOL

A Special Child in the Family
Living with your sick or disabled child
DIANA KIMPTON

Talking About Anorexia
How to cope with life without starving
MAROUSHKA MONRO

Think Your Way to Happiness
DR WINDY DRYDEN AND JACK GORDON

Trying to Have a Baby?
Overcoming infertility and child loss
MAGGIE JONES

A Weight Off Your Mind
How to stop worrying about your body size
SUE DYSON

Why Be Afraid?
DR PAUL HAUCK

You and Your Varicose Veins
DR PATRICIA GILBERT

You Want Me to Do *What*?
A guide to persuasive communication
PATRICK FORSYTH

Your Arthritic Hip and You
GEORGE TARGET

Your Grandchild and You
ROSEMARY WELLS

Overcoming Common Problems

SELF-DEFENCE FOR EVERYDAY

Practical Safety for Women and Men

Paddy O'Brien

Illustrated by Su Eaton

SHELDON PRESS
LONDON

First published in Great Britain in 1992
Sheldon Press, SPCK, Marylebone Road, London NW1 4DU

British Library Cataloguing-in-Publication Data
A catalogue record for this book is available from the British Library

ISBN 0–85969–645–6

Photoset by Deltatype Ltd, Ellesmere Port, Cheshire
Printed in Great Britain by Biddles Ltd, Guildford and King's Lynn

Contents

Note: The Law

Reasonable self-defence is no offence

What is reasonable?
Is the assault serious or life threatening?
(More than 90% of rape victims also think they are going to die)

Weapons

The carrying of any weapon or article purely to cause injury to or
incapacitate another is not lawful.

Acknowledgements

I would like to thank my Tae Kwon Do instructors: Meng Ken Too of Korea and Southampton, Mark Biddlecombe of Southampton, and Master Han of Korea and Slough, whose instruction has always been inspirational. I must also thank Inspector Peter Boatman who has shared his practical self-defence skills with me most generously over the last five years. Women and men who have attended classes of mine have all contributed ideas and shared thoughts and feelings, and Tim and the children have given love and support, as always.

1

Inner Peace

There is no doubt in my mind that the absolute core of good self-defence technique is a form of inner peace.

Perhaps the idea of learning some personal safety skills is an exciting new beginning for you. If you have picked up this book full of energy and enthusiasm and keen to learn self-defence methods themselves, turn straight away to the 'core technique' section of the book and work, learn, develop and feel exhilarated by that, and then return to this section when you are ready; when it crosses your mind to do so, or when you need a mental or a physical rest.

You may have picked this book up for quite a different reason and in quite a different frame of mind. You may have been beaten up or raped or frightened and abused, either recently so that the physical bruises still show, or a long time ago, so that the bruises and cuts no longer show on the outside, but are still there on the inside: in your inner self – your heart, or your soul, or your spirit – whatever word you use to name the core of your being. The bruises can stay there for a long time. Again, if this is why you are reading this page, feel free to choose for yourself which section you would like to start with. Take your time and choose what is right for you.

Another reason for investigating personal safety skills might be that you have suddenly become aware of the safety issue because of a violent incident at the office, an attack on a friend or family member, taking a new job or moving to a new area which creates a need to travel new routes, manage new locations and new types of clients or customers; or it might even be a news item which, because of some congruence with your own life makes you think: 'My god! it *could* happen to me'. You may have an urgent need to look at techniques first too. Do go ahead, call back in on these early pages when it is convenient and appropriate for you.

If you have a martial arts background you may find you *do* want to start here because it chimes in with the training you have already undertaken, to put your feet on the road of developing street-level personal safety skills via some good thinking about your inner equilibrium. This may have resonance for people in all sorts of other disciplines too.

1

If that is the case for you – begin here: after much thought it is where I want to start.

Competence in the Core Technique is 10 per cent theory and 90 per cent practice (see p. 21). But effectiveness in the core techniques, can, I feel, be multiplied many times over by moving towards an inner peace, because your body will be steady, integrated, and strong. The likelihood of your using your core skills accurately and in time will be multiplied many times over by attending to your own peace, because you will feel good enough about yourself taking up space on the planet, to know when it is essential to act to defend yourself. Your presence will not be victim-like and therefore hyper-vulnerable. Your strength and technical self-defence knowledge will be held within quietly and therefore not be provocative. Neither of those points ever made anyone *in*vulnerable though, and if you have already survived one or more attacks, or have to survive one in the future, access to a peace of your own is one of the most important resources you could have to heal and rebuild yourself with (see Figure 1).

We could look at a number of different ways of trying to develop and protect our own peace.

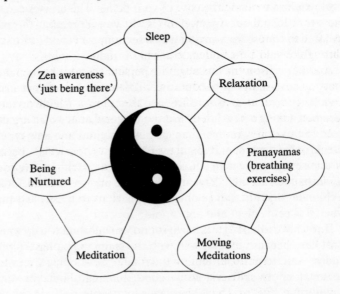

Figure 1

2

Sleep

Sleep that knits up the ravell'd sleeve of care
The death of each day's life, sore labour's bath,
Balm of hurt minds' great nature's second course,
Chief nourisher in life's feast.

Shakespeare *Macbeth*

Do you get enough sleep? Very many adults do not. Our extra-ordinary behaviour – commuting enormous distances, worrying compulsively about our work, compressing our free time into short frantic evenings, not getting much physical exercise, and generally embracing a pattern of life which is strangely mismatched with the needs of our animal bodies and our spiritual hearts – is highly disruptive of patterns of peaceful sleep.

Macbeth lost his ability to sleep because of his guilt about the murders he had committed out of ambition. We may lose sleep because of unease, guilt, worry, frustrated ambition, or physical imbalances (exhausted mind/alert body for example) but our loss is just as deep. Three hundred years before Freud, Shakespeare's description of the 'unravelling' power of a good sleep gives us the clue to why we need it so badly.

Every night of our lives we perform the creative act of dreaming away the unresolved conflicts of the day. Perhaps 'dreaming through' would be a better description than 'dreaming away': the resolution is by no means always complete, but our problems and frustrations are dramatized and illuminated by our dream cycles, and much healing and sorting out takes place. Whether you are fascinated by dream content and monitor and analyse it closely, or not, it happens anyway. In fact when you are so tense or preoccupied that you 'can't dream', the material that is worrying you is so pressing that your subconscious mind cannot clothe and disguise it sufficiently in dream imagery to allow you to deal with it by subconscious dream rather than conscious intellect, and there-fore to sleep.

The loss and disruption of dream-time and dream-clearance of problems helps to explain the desperation of some parents whose young children disturb them frequently at night. If you are in this part of your life, take seriously the extra demands it makes on you. If you are caring for the children with a partner, see if you can work out a rota which eases the needs of both of you for uninterrupted sleep. If this is not possible, take real note of the other peace-finding resources in this chapter and use them as much as you can as a substitute for enough sleep – to hold yourself together for the time being until you really can sleep well again.

Physical repair is part of the achievement of the sleeping body too. As well as 'knitting up the ravell'd sleeve of care', it is 'sore labour's bath'. Recovery from injury and illness is quicker in a body which is adequately rested, and the immune system is more effective.

The widespread use of antibiotics which knock bacterial illnesses out chemically, while without doubt a huge gain in survival and comfort, has inclined us to lose sight of the importance of rest in physical healing processes.

Review how much sleep you are having, and if it is not enough, take note of that. See if there isn't a way you could have a little more. If you do not sleep enough you cannot do the healing work of dreaming. Nor can your body make the physical healing and repair for which good rest is a requisite. The depression of chronic exhaustion erodes any attempts you make at well-being, fitness, and self-value. Think about sleeping well as being one of the components in your strategy of staying safe.

Relaxation

Relaxation techniques are part of the peace-finding cycle too. Relaxation can help you when you cannot sleep, either because you are being disturbed in the night, or because tensions have overwhelmed you. Short interludes of relaxation during the day can do a great deal to replenish your energies. An ability to follow a relaxation pattern can save a bout of insomnia from turning into a frantic tossing-and-turning panic attack; you can develop an ability to say to yourself: 'OK, I accept the fact that I cannot sleep. I shall do the next best thing which is to lie here and *relax*. Even though I cannot actually sleep I shall be resting in body and mind'.

Savasana

The basis of relaxation technique is yoga *savasana* or corpse pose. If 'corpse pose' sounds morbid to you, remind yourself that not all cultures have the same view of death as we do. It is not, to everybody, a negative finality: but it might be a peaceful transitionary time from one incarnation to the next, or from one mode of being to another, or it could be seen as a time where the elemental composition of the body is reabsorbed into the universe to be used in different ways. The point is that *savasana* or corpse pose is seen as a positive period of rest and re-creation, a brief sabbatical from the everyday push-and-pull of life.

The more you practise *savasana* the more you get out of it: relaxation is a skill (or an art) at which it is possible to get better as you become more familiar and skilled and perceptive about it. Either read through the suggestions for practice and become familiar with them (putting the book aside to try them out), or record them onto tape in a calm and steady voice, with a pause after each point. If you want to you can add some peaceful music onto the tape at the end of the instruction.

Practising savasana

Lie down on the floor on your back. Check that the centre line of your body is straight and your body evenly arranged around the spinal centre. On careful observation you may notice that your active and leading side (right for right-handed people and left for left-handed people) is contracted. Release it and feel your body spread symmetrically out from the spine.

Lengthen the back of your neck, pull your chin in a little to do this. If you feel you need to, slide your shoulder blades down towards your waist a little. Ease the position of your hips so that the arch under the small of the back is less pronounced.

Now, take your attention to each part of your body in turn. Take your awareness to your feet. Remember how they have carried you around all of your life! Breathing in, tighten up your feet a little, and exhaling, let them go. Relax your feet, feel them heavy and warm. Where they touch the floor, let them sink in a little more. Your feet will naturally roll outwards a little and be a little way apart. Your feet are heavy and warm.

Move your attention to your legs. Be aware of the strength of your legs, the muscles of calf and thigh, the long thigh bones, the knee joints, and the bones of the calf. Be aware of your legs. Inhale and tighten them. Exhaling, release them, let them go. Now take your thoughts to your hips, the centre of your fertility and sexuality, the centre of your strength and power for purposes of self-defence. Be aware of the strong arena of sensibility and power in your hips. Inhaling, tighten up your buttock muscles, pull your abdomen in towards your spine; exhaling, release and relax your hips. Let your hips feel warm, heavy, and relaxed, your abdomen soft. Think of the back of your waist spreading out.

If you need to adjust your shoulders again, then do. Take your thoughts to your hands and arms, the skills and strengths they have, the caring and pleasure they have given. As you inhale, tighten up your hands and arms, lift them a few inches off the floor. As you exhale, release your hands and arms. For now they do not have to do anything. Let them rest and be heavy. Your arms roll away from your body a little, your hands are soft and curved like a little child's. Take a deep breath in, fill your lungs up to the collar bones. Then breathe it away with a big sigh. After that, let your breath come and go as it wants to. It will probably settle into a light steady rhythm. Feel your chest and ribcage as relaxed, your heart warm and calm.

See if you can release your throat. As the brain chatters, the throat tightens. If you can let go in the throat, you can slow the activity of the mind. Keep the back of your neck long.

If your lips feel dry, moisten them with your tongue. Then let your tongue rest low down in your mouth, below the lower set of teeth. Let your lips feel soft, full and relaxed.

Frown gently, and screw up your eyes a little, then let your face relax. Let your eyelids rest lightly on your eyes, and the eyes feel heavy. Feel your forehead is smooth and cool. Your face does not have to express anything now. Rest it. Notice how the back of your head is heavy on the ground.

Your whole body is heavy and relaxed. Do not hold onto any muscles. You cannot fall through the floor. Let the floor do it all.

If you like to, take yourself off to somewhere you would really like to be in your imagination. It might be a warm, sunny beach, or a beautiful garden, or some favourite place in the countryside, or a sunlit or firelit room that you love. Choose anywhere that you feel particularly at home and at peace. Take yourself to your comfortable place in your imagination, and lay yourself down there for a rest.

[If you are making a tape, leave a long pause here.]

When you are ready to finish *savasana*, return slowly:

> Take some deeper breaths and yawn them out. Begin to stretch: small stretches first – stretch your fingers and your toes, stretch your arms and your legs. Remind yourself what your surroundings are before blinking your eyes open to take in the light. Do not sit up with a jerk. Bend your knees up onto your chest and roll over onto your side. Rest for a moment there if you want to, curled up in the position you slept in when you were very young. Press your hands into the floor and sit yourself up.
>
> Do not rush. Have a moment to notice the glow of peace and relaxation you feel before you return to the activities of the day.

Applications of savasana

A *source of peace inside* When you have done *savasana*, you realize that any peace that you feel, you have found inside yourself. It was there all the time; indeed, it *is* there all the time – and all that any of us needs is to know how to get in touch with it when we need it. There are many doors into this oasis of peace, and practice of *savasana* is one of them.

First aid for insomnia If you cannot sleep, accept it. Do *savasana* instead, and do it for its own sake alone. Sometimes you will fall asleep because you have done *savasana* and sometimes not, but anyway you will be resting well.

Stop flying the plane A common form of flying phobia is to feel that if you stop concentrating on 'flying' the plane, it will fall out of the sky. This creates acute tension. Many of us hold onto our lives in the same way. If we stop concentrating on surviving we think perhaps we will 'fall out of the sky'. This is not a stupid thing to feel. It is the result of living assailed and pressured lives. If you have survived assault and attack, you may have spent months or years 'holding on', 'holding yourself together', 'holding your feelings in'. *Savasana* gives us all a gentle, safe, uncomplicated way of experimenting with 'letting go'. Try it. Eventually the ability to 'let go' can spread into other bits of your life, as and when you are ready to let it do so. You

7

can find yourself crying while you do *savasana*. This is all right – it is another aspect of release. Your ears fill up with tears! Use some calm and soothing music to ease your sadness.

Two-minute savasana You do not have to lie down to move into that relaxed and useful space available in *savasana*. Once you are familiar with getting into that space you can do it for very brief periods in highly stressed situations. You might be having a horrific day in a hectic office, or caring for young children, or handling whatever the particular pressure of your daily life may be – whether it is dealing with an incessantly ringing phone, or doing a medical or social work task in an under-resourced, demoralized service, or performing, or being creative, or handling isolation, or developing new ideas. Any of those tasks and activities can be inspiring, but any of them can also be very demanding. You can give yourself a short visit to your own peaceful place.

Take two minutes – literally two minutes. Close the office door, or unplug the phone, or lie the baby safely in her cot and shut the door.

Sit yourself, equal weight in each hip, safely on a chair. Do the *savasana* contract-release sequence up through the body in a smooth flow like a wave flowing from foot to head. It only takes about 20 seconds. When you have done *savasana* before, you have visited a peaceful place which you visualized for yourself. When you do the two-minute relaxation, visualize a door – whatever sort of door comes into your mind. This is the door that opens into your peaceful space. After you have taken the wave of relaxation up through the body, visualize the door, and open it. Go straight through it into the peaceful place. Rest there, soaking up the sights, sounds, smells and the atmosphere, bathe yourself in the peace.

Return to your everyday space gently, being aware of your everyday surroundings before you blink your eyes open and take in the light. The couple of minutes you spend in the quiet place will have rested you, and put the problems surrounding you into a different perspective.

Breathing exercises

When the voice speaks, it is Life speaking.
When the eye sees, it is Life seeing.
When the ear hears, it is Life hearing.
When the mind thinks, it is Life thinking.
And when the breath breathes, it is Life breathing.

(*Kausitaki upanishad 111:1,2*)

Getting to know the way you breathe is another part of the generation of a pool of inner peace. It is strange that we may dedicate significant amounts of our time to improving muscle tone or paying attention to our weight, and indeed that we may learn all sorts of self-defence technique, and that we may put a great deal of effort into understanding and sorting our emotions out, but that we can forget that a basic activity that profoundly affects all these issues is our breathing.

We can live for days without food, and hours without water, but only minutes without breathing. How strange it is that we rarely practise to breathe better. Physical workouts and techniques are enormously improved when carried out with good coherent breathing. Steady breathing has a strong benificent effect on emotional equilibrium. This is a core part of yoga and martial arts philosophy and training and has a key part to play in the emotions around food, eating, and weight. It is used in a direct therapeutic application in a modern context by practitioners like Fiona Ashdown. For the past few years she has been mixing Desikachar Yoga sequences with transpersonal psychology and guided imagery in her classes in a large psychiatric department where she has been working with schizophrenics, manic depressives, alcoholics, and drug addicts. She feels that the focus on breathing is a major reason for the success of the methods she employs. As she says: 'So many people can't breathe properly. When they start to do so it has a powerful calming effect'. In a survey of the various different therapies on offer in that department, the patients and their families rated each method according to its effectiveness, and yoga, with its emphasis on rhythmic breathing, came out on top.

Try out these two different ways of breathing, and use them both as a pleasure in themselves and as a way to become more aware of the way in which you breathe generally.

9

Abdominal breathing Sit on the floor cross-legged. Support your spine, leaning against the front of the settee, or against a clear bit of wall (if such a thing exists in your house!) If your legs are not comfortable crossed, stretch them out in front of you, or find a comfortable position where your hips feel relaxed and open. If there is a friend around with whom you can practise, it feels great to sit back to back with another human being to try out breathing work. Not only does his/her spine support yours and yours support his/hers in pleasant mutuality, a delicious warmth seeps into your bodies from each other.

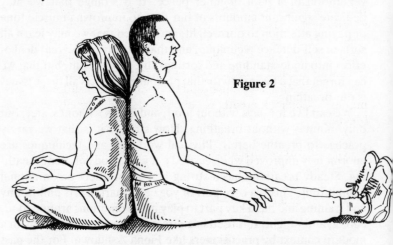

Figure 2

Once you are sitting and settled, lift your abdomen lightly and release your shoulders. Keep the back of your neck long and keep your face relaxed. Let your eyes close. Rest your left hand comfortably on your knee and your right hand on your lower abdomen, below the navel. Start to breathe a little more deeply and a little more slowly than usual. Hear your breath as it comes and goes in your throat. When your rhythm of breathing has settled, start to breathe in through your nose, and out through your mouth. Do not blow the breath out, simply part your lips and let the air escape.

When this cycle of breathing in through the nose and out through the mouth has become established, begin to become aware of your hand on your abdomen. Breathing in, your abdomen fills up so it swells under your hand a little. Exhaling, you empty, so your abdomen collapses back from your hand. The abdominal movement is slight – do not distend your abdomen out or crush it backwards – but feel a light action. This movement allows your lungs to fill and empty more fully. Notice on the inbreath how your lungs feel full and expanded not only up by your throat and collar bones, but also around near the sides of your ribcage and fully into the deep back of your ribcage. Notice on the outbreath how more stale air is cleared out from the lungs as you exhale fully.

This is how young children and young animals breathe naturally. If you can watch a baby's abdomen as he or she sleeps you will see it expand as the baby breathes in and deflate as the baby breathes out. Even though, as stressed adults, we may constrict our breath constantly into the upper chest – or even do the complete opposite to healthy breathing by sucking our abdomens in on the inbreath and flopping the abdominal muscles out on the outbreath – the proper abdominal breath is the way the body really wants to breathe.

When you are comfortable and easily breathing at this level, do two more things:

1. Hesitate a little between one breath and the next:

    breathe in – and hesitate –
    – and breathe out – and hesitate –

2. Start to even up the *length* of the breath in with the *length* of the breath out, and even up the *pace* of the overall breath. For example, if the inbreath takes a slow count of four, or seven, or ten, or whatever, make the outbreath last the same count. Visualize the breath as liquid, pouring into and out of the lungs and pour it in and out at an even rate.

    After a few minutes you will be ready to stop for the time being. Take your right hand away from your abdomen and rest it on your right knee. Let your breathing return to an everyday level, and become aware of the room around you, before blinking your eyes open to take in the light.

    Remain still for a few moments more to appreciate the peace and quiet which comes with this steady breath.

Whenever you feel threatened or angry or anxious or disturbed, try getting into this rhythm of breathing if you can – it is very helpful. Even if you needed a lighter and more ragged rhythm of breathing when you were in a tense or frightening predicament, this form of steady breathing is an enormous help for coping with the aftermath. It's simple: changing your breathing changes your mood and capacities. Use it like the relaxation *savasana* for short interludes during the day. When things are getting on top of you, take two minutes and breathe. It really makes a difference.

The exchange of gases occurring in your lungs is another point for reflection. There, deep in your chest is the interaction with other elements of the universe which plays a crucial part in keeping you alive. The world is moving in and out and through you all the time. Becoming aware of this increases your sense of connection with the world.

Alternate nostril breathing This form of breathing is useful for coping with insomnia, and panic too. Once again, when you become familiar with it, you can slip into it whenever you need to. Practise the breathing as follows:

Sit comfortably, cross-legged and with your spine supported. Rest your left hand on your left knee. Place the middle finger of your right hand between your eyebrows and then up slightly, on your forehead. Check that you can close your right nostril with your thumb and your left nostril with your fourth finger. As you get used to the rhythm, practise closing the alternate nostrils up with less and less pressure, eventually doing it as delicately as possible. To begin:

1. Inhale deeply
2. Close your right nostril with your thumb and exhale through your left nostril
3. Inhale through the left nostril
4. Close the left nostril with your fourth finger. Release your right nostril. Exhale through your right nostril
5. Inhale through the right nostril.

Repeat steps 2–5 steadily for a few minutes. Feel the breaths getting deeper and slower. Inhale and exhale at an even rate.

When you are ready to stop, finish a cycle and gently take your hand away from your face. Rest your hand on your right knee. Let your breathing return to an everyday level. Turn your eyes down so that you see the floor first and when you are ready, blink your eyes open and slowly get used to the light. Notice the sense of equilibrium that you feel.

Moving meditations

A moving meditation is any form of patterned movement which exercises and flexes the body and at the same time releases the brain from its continual inner monologue.

If you take part in dance or sport, weight training or yoga, skiing, running, marathon running, martial arts, swimming, or even simple walking, you will be well aware of the effects of moving meditation in your life.

Each different type of exercise of course has its own rhythm and its own feeling, and we are drawn in each phase of our lives to the things which match our needs and temperaments at that time. The point is that coherent patterns of movement requiring something between a little and a great deal of concentration, free the mind.

If your physical activity requires intense concentration because of a need for precision and safety, there is an obvious and immediate release from your everyday worries – there simply is not space to think about them. This mental release, and the fact that you have to dedicate yourself to getting the movements right, makes the activity into a moving meditation.

Even activities like walking or swimming, which flow easily and may not need intense concentration to stay on track, have an effect on relieving the clutter of the mind: the easy rhythm is soothing, productive of endorphins, and allows the mind to unclench and flow. That pleasant state of free flow of thought and the non-obsessive ability to solve problems and arrive at insights during activities like walking and swimming is a moving meditation also.

If your life has crowded in on you and squeezed out all space and time for physical activity, consider making space, if only once a week, for whatever kind of movement you feel drawn to at the moment. It is a great contribution to finding the inner peace we are considering in this chapter. If you fear that you are so exhausted that it would be impossible to manage anything physical, choose something very gentle and undemanding (for example, a little pleasant walking rather than marathon running), and you will notice that regular physical activity actually generates energy rather than removes it. This is another positive aspect of making sure movement has a place in your life.

If you are a survivor of violence there is another peace-making aspect in becoming involved in a physical activity. We often feel a paradoxical physical shame and degradation about being attacked, and can be left with a sense that our body is a disgusting object. This can be the case for men as well as for women, and can be true whether the attack involved a sexual assault or not – though this is not to say that the survivor of a sexual attack does not have extra distortions to their feelings about their own bodies to deal with.

One of the ways to begin to love your body again after an attack is to find a kind of exercise you like, which feels, not punitive, but reflective, exploratory, and strength-giving. This is another significant part that exercise – moving meditation – plays in our ability to make peace with and for ourselves.

Meditation

Meditation itself is a further element in our peace-seeking resource. Do not be put off by the esoteric aura surrounding the word. Meditation is simply noticing something that we all do spontaneously at times and making space and time to do it more often, as well as looking for techniques and practices that make it easier to do.

Meditation is what happens when the mind is completely clear. No thoughts, no mental events at all, intrude on a state of clarity and calm. It can happen spontaneously as you pass from daydream to reverie and from reverie to complete blankness. You might be sunbathing at the time, or in the bath; incense and the lotus position are not compulsory. (I do not mean to be flippant about incense and lotus. If they have been good aids for people to arrive at this beautiful state of mind when it has been difficult for them to do so, then they have served well. My point is that they are not always part of a meditative experience and nobody need be excluded from such experience because they do not like incense or cannot perform lotus posture.)

You can practise meditation deliberately as well as spontaneously.

Find a comfortable sitting position, preferably cross-legged, or, if that is too stressful, with the legs stretched a little way in front:

14

anyway with your hips as open as possible. Support your spine against the wall or the front of the settee or an armchair. Lift your spine and lengthen the back of your neck, and release your shoulders. Lift the abdomen lightly, and breathe steadily and rhythmically. Enjoy the breath.

Now tune into what is happening in your mind . . .

Probably it sounds like the concourse on Grand Central Station – myriad voices going on at once, massive exchange of information, announcements, anxieties, clear messages, indistinct messages, in short, chaos. This is why we need meditation so much – to make some spaces in between the chaoses.

The aim is to disperse all those voices, all those words, all those thoughts, all those questions, doubts, worries, and emotions, so that the mind stands clear, alone in itself. How is it done? There are many different ways – try some out and see what works for you.

Concentration on a single word, or sound, or object, may be a good way to reach a meditative peace. Using a word or *mantra* to clear the mind, is a very ancient practice. There are many *mantram* with different meanings, and if this form of meditation interests you, you can find out more about them in specialist yoga books.

A simple and fundamental mantra which anyone can use is 'ohm', the seed sound of the universe. Repeat it silently in your own mind, or if you like to, chant it. Make the open 'oh' part of the sound the closed 'm' part of it last the same amount of time, whether you work with it out loud or silently. When a thought or a worry or a plan intrudes, simply observe it, and then let it go. Little by little distracting thoughts come knocking on the door of your consciousness less and less, and a cool clear mental space appears. It is a wonderful feeling. Keep your steady flow of 'ohms' coming.

Eventually all worries disappear. Observe the peace. This is your peace, it was there inside you all the time. As with *savasana* the aim is simply to find out how to get in touch with it.

If you do not want to use a *mantra*, you could use a visual focus instead.

Find a shell, or stone, or flower that you like, or light a candle and

15

place it at a level that you can gaze at it comfortably as you sit in your upright, open-hipped position.

Once again, observe the inrush of thoughts in your mind, but gaze steadily at your flower, stone, candle flame – whatever you choose – blinking as often as is comfortable, and let that visual image fill your whole awareness. Let the rose, the flame, the shell, fills your entire mind – that is all that there is. When distracting thoughts tug at you, simply observe them, and let them go. Little by little they become less. Keep your gaze steady and let the beautiful visual image you have chosen gently fill your mind. Eventually no more distracting thoughts will come. Your mind is clear and free. Notice the sense of peace this brings.

Using a *mantra*, and using a visual focus, are good and simple ways to begin to learn how to meditate. It is not necessary to set yourself a target number of minutes per day, but just meditate when you feel a need to, and for as long as feels comfortable. Maybe it will only be for two minutes at first. That is fine. If you like the experience and find it does generate peace within you, you will want to do it more and sometimes may meditate for periods of half-an-hour or an hour; that is fine too.

Being nurtured

Navajo ceremonies are centred around the maintenance of harmony (as in the blessingway used at the birth of a new baby, the transition from girlhood to womanhood, or the blessing of a new hogan) or they are used, most commonly, to cure a person of a physical illness or a mental state, or bewitchment. Harmony and balance are essential to the Navajo: when a person has disturbed this harmony, even unknowingly, he or she will become ill . . . a cure can only occur through the proper ceremony (referred to as a chant, sing, or way) which in re-telling a portion of the Origin Story, symbolically recreates the world, and the patient. . . .

Gerald Hausmann *Meditations with the Navajo* Bear & Co.

The Navajo concept of recovery being linked with a method for re-making the self is what interests me here. If you have suffered literal and physical attack and assault, it is necessary to have a kind of re-birth, a re-making of the self, after the attack, which can lead to a kind of discovery. If you suffer from a more diffuse sense of assault, from living in a violent and uncaring and sexist culture, which most of us do, you also have a need to re-make yourself in order to feel able to go on, to feel able to face life day after day, to believe that the wounds this culture inflicts on you can be healed.

To cope with the violent and uncaring and sexist culture, our emotional defences are often up; to cope with having been raped, or beaten up, or threatened, or having felt threatened, our emotional defences are up. And this is often necessary. The sad loss though is that often when we are concentrating on not letting the bad things into our lives, our defences screen out the good things too.

It is absolutely necessary, in order to be strong, to be nurtured. You might be nurtured by other people and you might be nurtured by the world itself: the interesting thing is to begin to notice how that might happen, and to begin to let that nurturing in.

People may nurture us directly – by listening to us, talking to us, hugging us, feeding us, calming us, laughing with us, all the benign human interaction that goes with loving friendships from the lightest to the deepest contact. We need to be able to be open to how much that can re-create us. It means being open and therefore vulnerable. It means something which is important at a very deep level of self-defence, which is to know when you need to defend yourself and when you do not. In this way, developing a knowledge of self-defence and safety skills also develops your insight and intuition in personal relationships of any kind.

The people around us can nurture us indirectly too – by making it clear that we matter to them; that they value our skills or opinions or experience. And we need to learn to accept that nurturing – to avoid dismissing or devaluing compliments and positive feedback.

Of course there are periods in all our lives where the people around us do not nurture us at all, and we may be intensely lonely and isolated and suffer a terrible sense of exile. These times do make us feel bleak and vulnerable. We need particularly to take care of ourselves in every sense from the extreme of physical attack and assault to the detail of making ourselves as calm and comfortable as we can. A helpful way of beginning to do this is to allow the world to look after us a bit, by 'letting in' a clear awareness of how beautiful things are: the pattern of ice cracking on a puddle; the sudden wild scatter of starlings swooping round in formation looking for the night's roost; the pattern of clouds; the intricate shapes and colours of leaves; flowers; awareness of beauty in the world about us can really sustain us when we are feeling remote and unloved. This is not to romanticize away crumbling concrete, wrecked cars, and bruised lives. It is to say: you cannot help feeling the pain, do not forget to feel the beauty too.

Don't let the rapture pass you by
    (Robbie Robertson *Storyville* 'Soapbox Preacher')

Zen awareness: 'Just be there'

Zen is not a kind of mad extreme philosophy, although some of its practices and manifestations may look superficially odd to us in the urban industrial West. Zen, as I understand it, is an attempt to come to terms with the question of how to live, how to bear the pain of living, how to know what to do. It is special because it promises nothing, no reward, no guaranteed outcome, no gratification. What it does do is offer clues as to how to be fully alive in the present moment, which once achieved, can obviate a great deal of the anxiety and tension so common in our alienated lives. If you often feel restless and anxious it may be well worth finding out a little about Zen and how you could use it. It is not easy to put into words, but once you have grasped it, it is easy to feel.

In his book *Returning to Silence* Dainin Katagiri attempts to show what the oneness of Zen is by describing what happens when we swim – that the water and oneself are united in swimming or swimmingness:

> Two means the dualistic world. For instance, when you want to swim, there is the ocean and there is you. It is dualistic. 'Culminating in not-two' means jump into the ocean. Ocean and you become one. That is the ultimate state of becoming one. The oneness of the ocean and you is something active, something that leaves no trace of form . . . Being right in the midst of activity there is no form. All you have to do is just be there. This is oneness.

'Just be there' is the point to remember: as you try to soothe a baby with earache at four o'clock in the morning, as you sit on a train that has stopped in the middle of nowhere while the time of your meeting comes and then goes, just be there; as you experience joy or passion, just be there; as you struggle with fear, just be there; as you sit in your office stifled with boredom, just be there. Whatever is happening, just be there, just be fully present in it. When used in this way, this simple idea really does create an inner peace. It does not mean being passive, or stupid, or careless – it just means that when the real vividness of reality unfolding at 60 seconds a minute is felt clearly and 100 per cent by you, you feel a whole lot better about life. Just be there.

Talking of being bored, the Zen teacher Taknan gave this reply to a lord who found his diplomatic and official duties oppressively tedious:

> Not twice this day
> Inch foot time gem.

meaning: this day will not come again, each minute is worth a priceless gem.

The explorer Barry Lopez had an experience in Canada which has a Zen resonance. He describes spending time in a very lonely wilderness:

> The living of life, any life, involves great and private pain, much of which we share with no one. In such places as the inner gorge, pain trails away from us. It is not so quiet there or so removed that you can hear yourself think, that you would even wish to, that comes later. You can hear your heart beat. That comes first.
> Barry Lopez *Crossing Open Ground*

If you are already a student of martial arts, or if in the future you decide to become one, you will find that within the training the sheer repetition of learning basic technique and practising it over and over again, gives the long study a Zen-like quality:

> Karate-do is attained a step at a time, and so is life. Just train every day and try your best, and the truth will come to you.
> Ken Singleton *An Introduction to Karate*

Meanwhile aikidoist George Leonard makes the point about our modern restless un-connectedness:

> . . . there is simply no tradition in American culture for a longterm, strenuous practice that offers no specific payoff, no

guaranteed progress. Our best minds conspire to make everything painless, quick, and easy – 'Enlightenment in Ten easy Lessons'. Rewards are constantly dangled before our eyes: If you do *this* you'll get *that*. Even educational television programs strive desperately to be entertaining, diverting. If the audience is bored for as long as four seconds, for God's sake *do something*. After doing everything in our power to create short attention spans in children, we test them, and conclude that, yes, children have short attention spans. The notion of an attention span as long as a lifetime is foreign to us.

Strozzi and Heckler (eds) *Aikido and the New Warrior*

Leonard knows that the succession of ordinary aikido classes, week in and week out, is its own reward, and he knows too that to get through our life calmly, precisely what we need is an attention span as long as a lifetime.

If you look for activities and surroundings that enable you to 'just be there', your Zen awareness, together with all the other considerations described in this chapter, can form the inner peace which is at the core of your ability to stay safe.

2
Core Technique

People think themselves weak because they do not know how to use their strength.

Richard Chun *Tae Kwon Do*

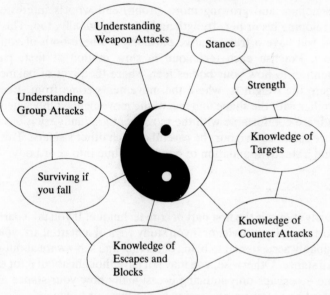

Figure 3

You may have chosen to start working with this book here. This chapter contains the nitty-gritty of physical technique (see Figure 3). The secret with physical technique is to practise it. It is 10 per cent theory and 90 per cent practice. However, do support your physical technique with work on inner peace, and with work on awareness.

With whom are you going to do your 90 per cent practice? Some of it you can do by yourself, familiarizing yourself with stances, movements, and sequences, but for a lot of it you will find you improve more quickly if you work with a partner. It is care in the choice of partners that is important. Sometimes people are tempted to begin their practice with a large, heavy, and aggressive partner because they feel it will be more realistic and that they need to find out whether their core technique 'really works'. This is not the most effective way to learn core technique: the risks are that if you feel weak to start with you reinforce a self-image of yourself as weak and victim-like, and that you become less rather than more in touch with your own power; furthermore, you may well hurt each other physically if, in the first instance, you go for a 'realistic' acting-out of the use of technique.

Instead, try to find a partner who has a real interest in you developing and growing more strong, and who is interested in developing his or her strength and power gradually, too. This way you will have a true creative partnership where both of you can grow. Practise each technique in slow motion at first, paying attention to how your bodies feel, where the pivot of balance is, where the weight is, where the movements come from. Become familiar with the shape and feel of the movements. Only when you both are comfortable with the movement gradually try it out with more speed and vigour, be careful of each other's safety. This will build a steady foundation of good technique into your body.

Stance

Steady stance is the first part of core technique. If you take part in a sport, or a dance style, or if you study yoga or a martial art, you are probably accustomed to being observant and self-aware about your own stance. Otherwise, you may not have thought about it for some time – perhaps only noticing occasionally how your stance alters according to your mood and your alertness or tiredness.

To keep your physical resources ready to help you with your personal safety you need a stance that:

- is difficult to knock over
- is easy to spring out from
- turns the vulnerable parts of your body away from an attacker.

Experiment with your stance in this way with two exercises.

Getting grounded
Working with a partner:

Stand around a bit! Experiment with standing in some of the different ways you know you stand in in everyday life. How do you stand in a queue? How do you stand when you are talking to your boss? How do you stand when you talk to a child? How do you stand in front of a class? If you have to make a public speech, or presentation, how do you stand? If you are making a complaint, how do you stand? With your partner share what those different stances are, what position you are in, where your weight is and how you are balanced, how comfortable or uncomfortable you are, and how much in or out of control of yourself and the situation you feel. Share too anything you notice about how different kinds of shoes might affect those positions and feelings.

Now try standing very stiff, straight and tall. Lock your knees straight, take your strength into your chest, lift your chin. Notice the similarity this has with Western military stance. Be aware of how you feel.

With gentle pushes, gradually increasing in force, let your partner try to push you off balance – from the front, from each side, from behind. Was it easy or difficult? Notice how it felt.

Change roles, and you try to push your partner off balance while s/he stands straight and stiff. Notice how it feels.

Now try standing in a different way. Place your feet hip distance apart and relax your knees slightly. Extend up through your spine, lengthen the back of your neck, and relax your shoulders down. Relax your arms and hands. Feel your centre of gravity in your hips. Be very aware of the strong contact of your feet with the floor.

Once again, let your partner try to push you off balance, first with gentle then with increasingly strong pushes. How does it feel? Is it easier than before, or more difficult?

Change roles, and try to push your partner off balance while he or she stands in the second way. How does it feel? Is it easier or more difficult? Now you have both tried both roles in both stances, talk to one another about the two experiences, and how they compared.

With this exercise, and with all the exercises in the book, always stay with what was true for you, and not with what the 'right' answer appears to be. If you did *not* feel what most people feel, you do not have to fake it. Power in you will grow from you being true to yourself, not from you conforming to what is supposed to happen – so you need to find out how you feel most safe in your stance.

Having said that, most people find the second way of standing, with the knees relaxed and the weight in the hips, the stronger option.

We need, then, to learn a new reaction to stress. Our primary reflex reaction may be to gasp air in and tense the body up, pulling the centre of gravity up to the chest – and as you have probably just experienced, this makes you rather easy to knock over. We need to learn to exhale, to release the knees, and to draw our strength into our hips. This makes us much more stable, much harder to knock over, and so much safer. This is the meaning of 'getting grounded'.

It is interesting to notice that Western military decoration – hats, epaulettes, medals – tend to emphasize upper body strength. Further, our idea of a 'strong' person tends to involve an image of a (male) person with heavily developed biceps, pectorals, and latissimus dorsi muscles – i.e. an emphasis on the top half of the body. For purposes of personal safety we may be more effective using the Eastern martial arts model of locating strength within the pelvis. The decoration in martial arts emphasizes this part of the body, using a white, coloured, or black belt, whose knot sits just below the navel at the spot where all powerful movement in martial art style originates from. The place is called *tan-tien* in t'ai chi, *tan-den* in karate and judo, and *dan-jun* in tae kwon do.

Originating movement from the pelvis gives it a whole-body power and a fluidity. Keeping the centre of gravity in the hips when you are static makes you difficult to knock over, and enables you to move quickly and accurately without losing your balance. It seems to me to be a healthier way to stand at any time, but certainly it is the best way to stand if you feel at risk.

If doing this exercise made you feel as though your hips were numb or inert, try it again – but circling, arching, flexing and rotating your hips a little from time to time. Many of us have been taught to keep our hips very locked because of the sexual connotations of being mobile and responsive in that area. Finding movement in the hips for purposes of self-defence may release all kinds of other material for you as well.

All work with the body is powerful in this way. Our biographies are written into our bodies, into our very bones and sinews, because our experiences of life shape the way we inhabit our bodies and the way we move around the world. Often, releasing a physical nexus that has been very tight and clenched brings great joy and relief. Sometimes it is upsetting because pain you have been 'holding on' to, starts to come out. If you feel distressed by this or any other 'letting go', look at Thérèse Bertherat's lovely book *The Body has its Reasons* (Cedar, 1976), which explores most sensitively the whole subject of physical 'holding' and 'letting go' of emotional pain. If the distress ever starts to feel like an emergency seek support without embarrassment, whether that means sharing with friends or looking for counselling or therapy. We all have darknesses to survive – there is nothing to be ashamed of in that.

All this proceeds from considering simply how one stands! How powerful such a simple choice can be, how wide the ramifications are!

Now that you are more aware of your stance, use the relaxed, alert, hip-centred stance whenever you can.

Sideways-on

If you ever feel at physical risk, exhale at once, and ground yourself in your hip-centred stance. If a source of danger approaches you, learn quietly to turn sideways on.

Practise first of all without a partner. Stand, in a grounded, hip-centred stance. Imagine a potential attacker moving towards you. As he gets closer, step one foot one small step back, so that you are sideways on to your attacker with your stronger leg in front. Keep your weight low. Notice which is the stronger leg? It is the one you would kick with automatically, before you stop to think about it. Try it out to see which it is. As you step back do not put one foot directly behind the other because this would make you rather unstable. Step the foot about a hip's width to one side as well. The front foot points forwards and the back foot points at 90° to the front foot (see Figure 4).

Even a small manoeuvre like this can feel difficult if you are not used to working with your body. Try to forget the issue of whether you are 'doing it wrong'. You are not aiming to 'do it right'. You are aiming instead to find a comfortable, relaxed, and powerful way to make this movement yourself. Just step back, then check: Weight low in the hips? Knees relaxed? Spine lifted? Shoulders relaxed?

Figure 4

When you can quietly take this step back without feeling flustered, practise with your partner.

Everybody has an area of 'personal space' around them, which they need to control. The boundary of that personal space varies according to the person you are relating to. The people closest to you can come right into skin-to-skin contact with you without you feeling intruded upon, but you may still need to negotiate about how much time they spend there! Close friends can move physically quite close and make occasional physical contact without you feeling invaded. People you know less well need to be at a greater distance (say three or four feet away rather than eighteen inches away), for you to remain comfortable. If somebody seems hostile or threatening you need them to be much further away in order to feel safe – maybe three or four yards.

26

Ask your partner to go right across the room from you, and to start slowly to walk towards you. As soon as s/he gets to a place where you start to feel s/he is 'too close' – i.e. your personal space is beginning to feel invaded – without any fuss at all, turn sideways on. And check: Knees relaxed? Centre of gravity in the hips? Spine lifted? Shoulders relaxed?

Repeat this exercise several times. Vary the moment at which you move into sideways stance by imagining more or less threatening circumstances and approaches. Step back neither surreptitiously nor exaggeratedly. Think of being calm and alert. When you have had half a dozen goes, change roles and you approach your partner, allowing him or her the opportunity to experiment with when to step back into a sideways stance.

When you have both worked on sideways stance, have some time to talk about how it feels to be both the approacher and the approached. Notice particularly what happened *vis-à-vis* eye contact. It is important to maintain eye contact with your partner as s/he approaches, and to work out how it feels to look with a calm and determined gaze; not a victim gaze and not an aggressive gaze. If someone moves towards you in a threatening manner, it is tempting to look away, but it is important to learn to keep your eye on him or her. If actual eye contact is intimidating, focus on another part of the body, but do not look away . If any other dangerous object was moving towards you, you would be careful to keep it in your sights. Do the same with a potential attacker: 'Don't take your eye off an oncoming train'.

Finding your strength

How are you to find the strength you need to defend yourself? How can you cope if you are attacked by somebody much heavier or stronger than you?

There are various ways into this question. The key is to understand that there is more to strength than weight and muscle-to-muscle opposition. If you are heavy and strong, you may be able to use those qualities to help yourself, but you have other resources at your disposal too. If you are light or not muscular you can still be very effective in staying safe. Your extra resources are:

• Knowledge and accuracy

- Self-knowledge and determination
- *Ki* – resilient strength

Knowledge and accuracy means the precision and technique you are working on in this chapter. Self-knowledge and determination are absolutely crucial and are discussed fully in Chapter 3. *Ki* or resilient strength is the subject of the following exercise. If you are a student of martial arts you will be familiar with resilient strength by the name of *ki* or *chi*. If you are a student of yoga you will be familiar with resilient strength by the name of *prana*. Finding resilient strength in yourself is finding the *ki*, the *chi* or the *prana*. It is there inside everybody; it is unlocking a potential that is already there.

With your partner: stand facing one another, both with feet hip-distance apart. Place your right arm on the left shoulder of your partner (see Figure 5).
First of all feel tense and muscular strength. Clench your fist, palm facing upwards, tighten up your arm muscles, lock the elbow. Now ask your partner to place both hands on your elbow

Figure 5

joint and to start to press down on the joint. S/he should continue to press down on the joint until your arm bends. Notice how it feels and how much strength is needed to bend your arm.

Shake your hands and arms and rotate your shoulders and hips a few times to release the tension in your body and then try again another way.

Once more, face your partner; once more, rest your left arm on his or her right shoulder, palm upwards. This time, however, do not clench your fist. Relax your knees, and feel your feet firm on the ground, your footprints broad and even. Feel your centre of gravity in your hips. Steady your breathing. Imagine strength flowing into your body from under the ground; flowing through the soles of your feet and up into your legs and hips. Imagine the strength flowing up into your torso and along into your extended arm, which seems to be longer and longer, which seems to extend for ever. Some people imagine the strength flowing like water through a hose up through the body and out through the arm. Others visualize it as an electrical charge or a coloured glow. See it as whatever feels real to you as a source of flowing power.

Keep your breathing steady and your knees relaxed. Once again, ask your partner to put his or her hands on your elbow joint and gradually to put increasing pressure on it to bend it. As you feel the pressure, focus on the idea of the power flowing through you, of your arm extending and extending. If that feels easy, you may find you can absorb some of the energy they are using to press down with, to add to your own energy. If you start to tense up, simply remind yourself to breathe steadily, keep your knees relaxed.

Notice how it feels this time. Notice how much pressure it takes to bend your arm.

Then change roles: this time your partner tries out the two different kinds of strength, and you try to bend his or her arm.

When you have finished take some time to talk about what it felt like. The chances are that you found the second time, when you used resilient strength, that there was far more strength present in your body than you could have guessed. Without getting any fitter or heavier or more muscular: there in your body as it is now was strength. You simply accessed it when it is normally blocked. This fluid, relaxed, resilient strength is the strength you need in your development of personal safety skills. Certainly, you may choose to build up fitness, stamina, and flexibility as well, but this resilient strength is your key resource.

If you did *not* experience the second, resilient and relaxed arm position as more powerful, do not feel you have to fake it. It is not working or flowing for you at the moment, that is all. Try again on a different day, or try again when you have covered other parts of the core technique, and you may experience that flow of *ki*. Never fake it, since being safe in your own body means being true to your own feelings about your body however many layers of conditioning you have to peel off to do so.

Knowledge of body targets

Why should you want to step into a sideways stance when a threatening person approaches you? The reason is twofold: first, you have your front (stronger) leg and both your hands ready to defend yourself with; second, you turn most of your body's vulnerable targets away from your attacker. The following and subsequent exercises will make those points very clear.

Let us start by considering what the body targets are. There are vulnerable points on your body and there are vulnerable points on anybody else's body, and they are more or less the same. A 17 stone man is vulnerable in more or less the same places as you are, and a heavily muscled body builder is, too – as is somebody who is drunk or drugged (although we do need to take into account that their perception of pain will be different), and so is somebody who is sinister or looks weird or is wearing a mask, or making strange or frightening noises. Their body still operates in more or less the same way and you can act on that knowledge to overcome all sorts of intimidation and violence. These are the vulnerable points on anybody's body (see Figure 6).

A well-directed blow to any of these points on an attacker's body will cause enough pain and inconvenience to cause him (or her) to move his attention from you to himself.

Learn the target points with your partner. Take turns to point out all of the body targets which you can remember on each other, until you both remember the full set right through.

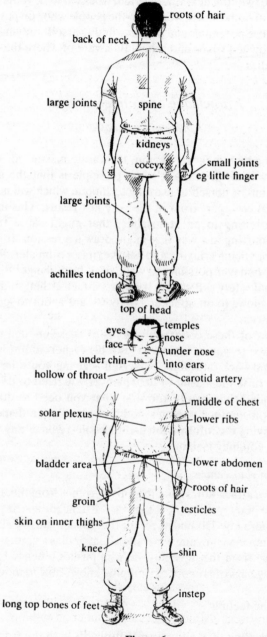

Figure 6

Take time over the next few days and weeks to look at the people around you at home and at work, and the people who you pass in the street or whose physiques you perforce find yourself studying as you travel on crowded trains and tubes. Be aware of where the targets on their bodies are.

Knowledge of counter-attacks

Karate ni sente nashi

This teaching by Funakoshi Gichin, the karate master, means: 'In karate there is no first attack'. The principle is that the student dedicated him- or herself to learning technique which will never be put to actual use apart from in the very last resort. This includes never contributing to an atmosphere that might cause trouble, never even moving in a way that might draw aggression. It is quite different from being cringing and passive: it is a calm alertness and an ability, whenever possible, to walk away from danger.

In personal safety skills there is no first attack either, and all the strikes and blows to an attacker's body we are about to learn are counter-attacks.

The object of these counter-attacks is to cause enough pain or inconvenience to your attacker to take his or her attention away from you and back onto him- or herself – giving you time to run away, or to raise the alarm, or do whatever you need to do.

You will find that simply knowing what you need to do to act effectively on another person's body, changes your demeanour anyway. Having the information and the skills reduces any victim-signals that you may give out.

Moving from your centre

Any effective attack flows from the hips; it comes from the 'tanden' centre of the body, just below the navel. All dancers, sports people, can do this already. Do not be afraid that it is an elusive skill that you cannot manage: anyone who sails a boat or digs a garden knows how to move from the hips; anyone who pushes a heavy pram or carries heavy bags of laundry or shopping knows how to move from the hips.

Try out the feeling:

Stand tall, then take a long stride forwards with the front knee bent. Keep the spine upright and push your hands out in front

Figure 7

(see Figure 7). Feel your hip centre.

Then step back to the centre and draw the hands back towards you. Step out again a few degrees to the left, extend out strongly, and feel control in your hips. Then step back again, draw yourself back to your centre. Continue moving round a few degrees until you have stretched and extended your energies in a circle all around you. Think of keeping that feeling in your body while you learn your counter-attack.

Striking through the target

To deliver an effective counter-attack you need to learn to strike *through* a target. Unless you have considered this you tend to hit *at* the target so that almost all of the energy of the strike is used up by the time of impact. If you actually aim at a point several inches *behind* the target, you make a strike which hits while it still has plenty of potential energy, and drives effectively through.

Try this out with your partner:

Stand facing one another and ask your partner to stretch his or

33

her arm out to the side at shoulder level, hand open and facing you. Mime a punch to your partner's hand to make sure you have got the distance you need. Now try a few punches aiming *at* the hand. Ask your partner to relax in the shoulder so that his/her arm swings back with the impact of the punch so it does not hurt. Notice what kind of impact you can make with punching 'at'.

Do not be disheartened if you miss your target altogether at first. Unless you practise an activity where eye-hand coordination is developed, it can be difficult to begin with. Just keep trying. Take your time and do not rush.

After a few goes of aiming *at*, try aiming *through*. Aim your punches at a point a few inches behind the hand of your partner. See what kind of difference this makes to the effectiveness of the punch – i.e. see how much further your partner's arm swings back. Take care to control the punch so that you do not hurt one another.

Next, change roles and allow your partner to try out the difference between punching *at* and punching *through*. Take a few minutes to talk together about how it feels.

Keep your sense of striking *through* in all your practice of counter-attack techniques.

Strikes to targets

Just one more point. You may begin to feel very squeamish when you start to realize just how much you can hurt someone, and you may begin to feel that you are not prepared to do certain things to another person, no matter what. Everyone has to reflect within himself and decide what his personal limits are. Remember though – you are not learning these techniques because you think it would be fun to go out and hurt people; you are taking the trouble to acquire these skills because you want to know how to be more safe.

With that in mind, let us match a strike or strikes to each vulnerable body target.

The eyes

Most people will move back on reflex from a determined movement towards their eyes. If you land an attack on someone's eyes the eyes will water copiously, vision will be blurred and the person will feel quite enough pain to want to sort things out rather than rush after you. At a distance you can make a counter-attack to an attacker's eyes with a double-eye poke (see Figure 8).

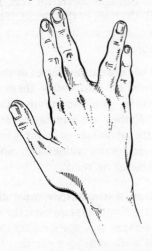

Figure 8

Double-eye poke If your hand easily organizes itself into this arrangement use it. If not, simply use your second and third fingers. Practise taking a lunging stride forwards and thrusting the right hand from beside your waist out and forwards to an imaginary attacker's eyes, then stepping back and drawing your right hand back to your waist. Try this several times. Start in slow motion, then gradually build up speed and power. With a partner, try out a double-eye poke towards the eyes. Notice how uncomfortable it makes him/her feel even though you both know you will not actually touch. *Remember*: if you use this manœuvre for real you must aim, not *at* the eyes, but *through* the eyes; at a point a couple of inches behind them. Change roles and see what it feels like if someone makes a determined movement towards your eyes.

Double-eye press If you are struggling at close quarters with an attacker you may be able to use a double-eye press.

Place your hands on either side of the attacker's head, place a thumb on each eye, and press. With a partner, try out the hand positions, but only press extremely lightly on their eyes. Let them try it on you too and register how very uncomfortable it is.

If you need to use this manœuvre for real, press the attacker's eyes firmly towards the back of their head. If the thought of doing this appals you, remind yourself that you are learning these skills in order to live more safely.

What if your attacker is wearing glasses or sunglasses? If you are close in, take them off and throw them away. If they are prophylactic spectacles, you gain the advantage of reducing your attacker's vision. If they are sunglasses worn to prevent eye contact, you gain the advantage of possibly making your attacker more humanized and more vulnerable, and his or her facial expression is also easier to 'read'.

This raises the question of whether you wear glasses yourself, and would feel very helpless if your glasses were thrown away. If this is a predicament which you fear, it is worth taking some time to do some sensitive and gradual work with your partner. Experiment on how you can manage your techniques without your glasses, and how you can use your sense of touch to work out where your attacker's body targets are and how to deliver effective counter-attacks to them. Many people find that, once the initial panic subsides, they are surprisingly competent without their glasses. Clearly it is very useful to get through that initial panic, and to get some sense of how you can and do cope without your glasses, in a controlled and safe situation. You are then far better equipped to cope should this ever happen during an attack.

The upper lip

Y-hand strike You can make an effective strike to the area between the upper lip and the base of the nose with your hand arranged in a Y-shape:

Stretch the thumb away from the fingers on the right hand. Keep the fingers together. The point of contact is in the point of the Y – the area between the root of the thumb and the root of the index finger.

Practise, in slow motion at first, then building up speed and power, making a Y-hand strike. Start with your hands in loose fists at waist level. With a long stride forwards, thrust the right hand forwards and out, clearly visualizing your attacker, and visualizing the target between his/her upper lip and the base of the nose. Remember to visualize striking right through that target for optimum impact. Become familiar with this movement on your own, and also practise stepping towards your partner with a Y-hand strike, making quite sure that you do not make actual contact with them with the technique. Let him or her practise stepping towards you with a Y-hand strike too, so you have an idea what it feels like to have it coming towards you. Try out the technique with both hands, and see which feels more powerful.

You have probably knocked yourself accidentally on this upper-lip area at some point. You will remember that a sharp knock here makes your nose and eyes run and is surprisingly painful; a rather sharper knock easily causes the nose to bleed, and the pain is quite intense. It is distracting and uncomfortable enough to be a valuable self-defence technique.

The chin

Palm thrust A useful counter-attack to the chin is palm thrust. To practise palm thrust, first of all find the appropriate hand position:

Keep your fingers and thumb close together, then pull your fingers back slightly and curl them. Curve the thumb. Push the heel of the hand forwards and out. The point of contact is the heel of your hand. You are going to push the heel of your hand firmly up and under and through your attacker's chin.

Practise once again by making the palm thrust, starting with your hand at your waist, then taking a long stride forwards and thrusting the hand forwards. Visualize clearly pushing up under your attacker's chin. Start slowly and build up speed and power. Practise with your partner, being careful not to make contact. Let him or her practise with you and see how it feels having this strike travelling towards you. Become familiar with making a palm thrust with both hands.

A firm palm thrust under the chin causes your attacker's head to jar backwards very uncomfortably. It is also likely that he will bite his tongue, which can be painful and distracting. The palm-thrust is a very useful counter-attack if you are shorter than your attacker or if you are in a grip underneath him. Remember that you need to think of pushing right through the chin to a place a few inches behind it.

Throat

Tiger-mouth-hand If you are close in to your attacker you may be able to make a counter-attack to his/her throat: everybody's throat is a very vulnerable area. Learn how to make a tiger-mouth-hand strike to the throat.

Figure 9

First of all, work out the hand position: Fingers and thumb are curved inwards, ready to spring together in a pincer movement (see Figure 9).

Next, work out where the critical point on the throat is: feel your own throat and your partner's. Some people really hate having their throat touched at all. If you are very sensitive around the throat, just feel your own throat. Find the Adam's apple – in a woman it is a small swelling around the windpipe, in a man it is much more clear and pronounced.

You are going to take your tiger-mouth-hand up to this point and press forward firmly into the neck with your fingers and thumb, then spring your finger-tips and thumb-tip together as though you are trying to make them meet round the back of the windpipe. When you practise with your partner, only do it very gently indeed. Even a gentle squeeze will make you cough, splutter, and withdraw: so you can tell that if you did it with full commitment it would create a big impact.

Practise, as before, starting with the hand in at the waist, and stepping forwards with a lunging step, visualizing the attacker's throat as you close your tiger-mouth-hand on it. Practise close in with your partner, but take care to control the technique. Get familiar with doing the technique with either hand.

The face

Side punch Unless you have been doing forward punches all your life, or you study boxing or martial arts, a front punch can be an awkward manœuvre. A side punch, in contrast, is easy to learn and has the advantage of utilizing an easy centrifugal force. A side punch can be aimed effectively at the face of an attacker if you need a general counter-attack.

Learn to side punch this way:

Make a fist curling your fingers and tucking your thumb on top of the bent fingers. If you leave your thumb sticking out it can get damaged easily; if you tuck your thumb inside your fingers it will be damaged if you do make an impact with it, so be sure your fist is safe.

Stand sideways on to your target with your right foot in front. Relax your knees, and take your centre of gravity down into your hips. Cross your right arm across your chest, then, in slow motion, throw it out towards the target. Do this again until you can make the movement with ease and accuracy. You are aiming to go right through the target of the face. Practise with your partner, pulling the punch just before it lands, so as to get a sense of distance and focus. Work carefully and sensitively together so that you gain experience without accidents.

You can feel the centrifugal force in the swing of the punch. Become familiar with using both arms to do this technique.

The mid-section of the body

The area from the shoulders to the hips is the mid-section of the body. It is pointless to hammer on the hard surfaces of an attacker's chest, and you may feel that you are not confident enough to land an effective push or punch to the solar plexus, or a good enough blow to the lower abdomen, and if so you may want to concentrate on other counter-attacks which may be sharper or more surprising.

However, if you decide you do want to work on counter-attacks to the mid-section try the next technique.

Open palm push Locate the solar plexus and, moving energy on your attacker from the hip-centre of your body out along your arm, give a firm push *through* the solar plexus.

Try this out with your partner, starting with gentle pushes, and working out gradually just how far you can shift them with a relaxed, firm push. Change roles and receive the pushes this time, and be aware of what your partner is doing when s/he makes her/his most effective pushes.

Low punch An effective blow to the lower abdomen is a useful counter-attack because it can cause your attacker to be winded, and possibly double over and bring his/her face close to you as another potential target.

Practise a low punch by making a safe fist as in a side punch (see p. 30) with your right hand, then pulling your right hand in to your waist. Swing it out in an arc and round towards the imagined target of the attacker's lower abdomen. Remember your punch has to swing right *through* the target, not land on it. Try the movement out with your left hand too, and work out which you think is more comfortable for you.

Then, with a partner, ask him/her to extend an arm out to the side, hand extended and palm facing you, and aim some punches at or through this target. You can also try asking your partner to hold a cushion over his/her lower abdomen and aim some low section punches at this. Start slowly and carefully and build up speed and power. Take care not to hurt your partner, once your punch is focused; the impact, even through the cushion, can be uncomfortable.

Exchange roles and see what it is like receiving the punches. When you are the partner receiving the punch, stay relaxed in your knees and centred in the hips, and move back if you need to.

The testicles

If your attacker is a man, you can make a devastating counter-attack to his testicles.

Grip the testicles and twist them, or bring a sharp blow up and under the testicles. Your attacker is going to be in extreme pain, out of breath, in some degree of shock, and not able to walk or run comfortably for a good 15 minutes. In most cases this is plenty of time for you to extricate yourself from the situation completely.

Again, you may find you feel revolted at the prospect of using this counter-attack. Remind yourself that you are working at how to do this because you are in a dangerous culture where, at times, your life may be put at risk by another person; you are not doing this because of any sadism in you. You need to know what your options are, and, of course, then whether you use them is always up to you.

No man is ever going to let you practise this manœuvre on him. Simply remember that you need to make a decisive movement and to get right *under* the testicles: hitting someone on the pubic bone in the *front* of the body hurts very little and gives warning of your intention.

The knees

The knee joint is very vulnerable and is a good site for a counterattack. An adult leg kicking accurately delivers more than six times the force needed to break someone's knee. An attacker whose leg is badly hurt will withdraw his or her energy into him-/herself, and will also be unable to move quickly or to run after you.

If you do the all-purpose warm-up regularly (see p. 91), you will find yourself becoming increasingly flexible, especially a growing mobility in the hip joints, and a lengthening in the hamstrings. Once this happens, your legs can become marvellous weapons. If, eventually, you choose to study tae kwon do, or karate, you can learn to flick completely unexpected kicks up to head-height.

Side-stamp kick With some work on flexibility, and with some work on accuracy, you can produce a kick which is good enough to be a strong counter-attack (see Figure 10). The shape of the kick is this:

Step easily back into your sideways stance. Your knees are relaxed and your centre of gravity is in your mobile hips. Bend your front knee up, as high as is comfortable. Lean slightly towards your bent knee in order to keep your balance, and to pull your energy into your centre. Now, in slow motion, stretch the

41

Figure 10

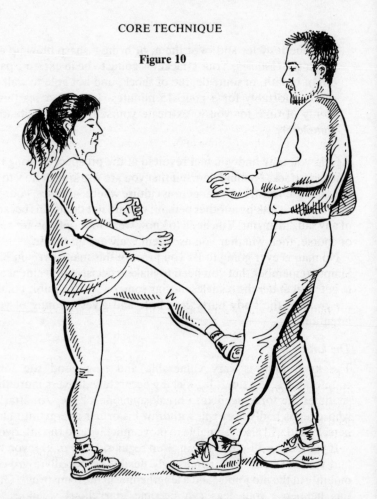

leg down in a kicking movement. The outside edge of your foot is the main point of contact with the target (the whole foot quickly follows, but think of landing the outside edge of the foot first). Repeat several times slowly, then gradually increase in speed and power. Visualize what you are doing: think of stamping right through that attacker's knee.

Work with the other leg too and decide which is the most comfortable and effective side for you.

If you work on a physical discipline you will be aware of the importance of symmetry and be keen to develop equal skill on both sides. If, however, you are looking at how you can acquire safety skills with a minimum of extra investment of time, use your 'natural' strong side all the time.

Useful practice with your partner on side-stamp kick is to repeat your 'sideways stance' exercise, (see p. 25) where the 'attacker' approaches you, and you, calmly, turn sideways-on. Imagine that this is a threatening approach which you feel it would be dangerous not to stop. As the attacker comes within range, with your front leg do a side-stamp kick down onto their knee. Pull the kick so that you do not make any contact with your partner at all; make sure you do not accidentally hurt them. Walk through the sequence slowly at first then gradually speed up, but continue to control that 'live' kick so that you do not hurt your partner. Notice how, if you follow the kick through, your attacker's head is brought towards you and you might want to follow up with a side punch (see p. 39).

Change roles and practise again, observing what works and what does not work.

The side-stamp kick works well to the back of the knee as well. Once you are looking at the back view of any attacker you have the situation in control anyway, and there may be no need to do anything more: but if you are dealing with a group, or if you feel you need to make a further counter-attack, try stamping down hard, with the technique you have worked on, onto the back of the knee joint. At least he will lose his balance, and may well completely fall over.

Pushing kick A pushing kick is a useful counter-attack and another kicking technique for your repertoire. It is performed with the flat of the foot (see Figure 11).

Stand in the sideways stance. Pull your front knee straight up towards your chest, leaning in towards your knee. Thrust the flat of your foot towards the target – which is the solar plexus on the front of an attacker, or the coccyx on the back – and push *through*. Keep your momentum going forwards. This simple kick will unbalance and often easily knock over an assailant. You can practise with your partner, with control, both doing, and being on the receiving end of a pushing kick.

43

Figure 11

Using your voice

The use of the voice is the link between the knowledge of counter–attacks, and the knowledge of blocks and escapes. Your voice is a powerful resource!

You could use your voice in an attack or assault or threatening situation, by being assertive; in negotiation or persuasion, by being fierce or cunning.

What we want to look at here is how you can learn to use your voice as a weapon, or as a way to enhance your body weapon techniques. In karate there is a shout called *kiai* and in tae kwon do the equivalent shout is called *kiup*.

The first character *ki* is the symbol for spirit, mind, energy, force. The second character *ai* is the symbol for meeting, or coming together. 'The coming together of mind' – *kiai* is a convergent laser of awareness and action

from C. W. Nichol *Moving Zen*,
Karate as a way to Gentleness

Shouting with a counter-attack increases its ferocity, its physical power, and its psychological impact. It establishes your will and determination with regard to your own survival.

If you sing, or chant, or act, or speak a great deal at work – for instance if you teach or work mainly via a series of discussions or meetings – then your voice is probably well-centred and strong and you have some idea of its range and scope.

If you feel embarrassed or uncertain about your voice, it might take a little bit longer to get hold of its true power.

Voice warm-up

It is helpful to warm up the voice, just as we always take time to warm up the body. In the case of an emergency, just as with your body, adrenaline will do the job for you.

Sit with your spine supported – against the wall or against the front of a sofa or armchair. If your partner is with you, sit back-to-back as you did for the breathing exercises (see p. 9).

Cross your legs or, if that is uncomfortable, stretch your legs out in front. Lift your spine, lift your abdomen, and relax your shoulders. Lengthen the back of your neck and stretch the crown of your head up towards the ceiling. Rest your hands comfortably on your knees or in your lap.

Close your eyes and settle into a slow and steady rhythm of breathing. When you are ready, on your exhalations start to make a humming 'mm' sound. Choose any note you like. Choose any volume of sound you like. Just hum. Notice where in your head and body you feel the sound vibrate.

After you have had a few 'mms', change to these other sounds in turn: 'oo', 'ee', 'ah' and, lastly, 'oh'.

Change pitch and volume as you like. Be aware with each sound where it resounds within your body. Notice how the breath and the sound get deeper and longer as you continue.

When you have tried each sound for a while, let your breathing return to an everyday level. Become aware of the room around you before blinking your eyes open to let in the light.

Although it may feel peculiar at first, once you relax you will find this strangely soothing and relaxing. In workshops, even groups who start off thinking they will choke with embarrassment if they have to make unstructured sounds, will relax after a few moments into chanting strange and beautiful harmonies. Taking time to 'play' with your voice like this from time to time will develop and deepen its qualities.

Learning to shout

What words might you want to shout if you were threatened or attacked? Maybe 'Help!' or 'No!' or 'Go away!' Try shouting, *really* shouting, the words you feel you might use. When can you do this? If you are not in a class or group, try shouting while you are driving your car, or while you are using a noisy machine (drill, hoover, cassette player), or warn your neighbours you are going to make a tremendous noise and let rip! See just how much noise you can make. Shouting loudly at someone calls attention to your predicament. Pitching it deep and extremely loud can alarm your attacker and alert others. A loud roar may be all you need to do to get rid of him or her.

If shouting isn't enough, and if you need to make an escape (see p. 49) and a counter-attack, try a yell *with* the technique. It focuses your energy, makes the technique more powerful in itself, and is very disconcerting for your attacker. When you practise, try yelling sometimes to get used to how it feels and sounds. Find the fierce animal within you: you will have your own personal snarl, roar, or growl. Let it out and make friends with it, it can be very useful to you!

Two further points about shouting need our attention. First, there may be some words that you notice are very difficult for you to shout. One man spoke at a personal safety training session about shouting the word 'Help!' He said: 'As a man, I am supposed to know what to do. I feel I can't cry out for help to other people. I ought to be able to control the situation on my own.' Many men share his feeling that they ought to be endlessly strong and resourceful and ought to be able to handle any kind of physical threat through some sort of intrinsic knowledge. It would have a profound effect on both men and women for men to begin to be able to use the word 'Help!' when they want to.

Similarly, anyone who has been sexually abused as a child or pressurized over sex as an adult, or been raped, may find it difficult or painful to say or shout the word 'No!'. In the short term, learn to yell other words or phrases in an emergency, such as 'Go away!', or

'Get out!'; but think too about beginning to use that word 'No', when *you* want to.

Just as making new kinds of physical movement can release emotional trauma held in the body, saying words long unsaid can release emotional trauma from the verbalizing part of the mind. With support, if you want it, think about allowing yourself, in your own time, to do that.

The second point is whether your mouth will dry up completely if you are scared, making it difficult to make any sort of noise at all. You may be frightened of this because it has actually happened to you in the past, or because it seems all too likely in theory. Well maybe it will, in which case you cannot use your voice until your saliva starts to flow again – and you have to use your other resources in the interim. However, you can make it a lot less likely that your voice will dry up on you by thinking always of converting fear into anger into energy, or thinking just how loud you would be able to shout if you needed help for your child or loved one, and getting hold of all that power and volume on your own behalf. This point is covered further in Chapter 3.

Knowledge of blocks and escapes

Blocks

If a blow is coming towards you, your first choice option is to get out of the way of it altogether by stepping back or sideways out of range, or by running away. The second line of defence of blocking is necessary if you are stuck at close quarters, or did not have time to get out of the way. Get into the sideways stance facing the oncoming attack, and use your arms to intercept the blow.

Practise:
a) Low block which protects the waist-to-knee area
b) Inner and outer blocks which twist and protect the chest and upper chest
c) X-block which protects the face and neck
d) Upper block which protects the face and head (see Figure 12)

Follow the movements from a to d, first in slow motion, then with increasing speed and power. Combine them with moving into the sideways-on stance. With your partner, work on your blocking technique. Ask him or her to move towards you as

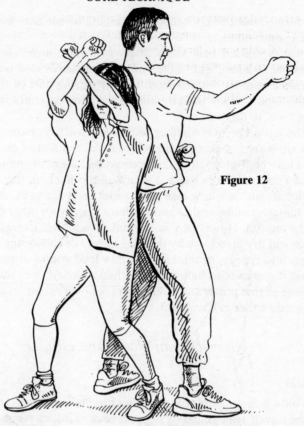

Figure 12

before. When you feel you need to, turn sideways on. Your partner should mime an attack to one of the four areas above, and you should practise blocking it. Do it in slow motion at first, gradually speeding up as you improve your skill in reacting, but continue to take care of each other. If you get too fast and exhilarated you may hurt one another. Be aware of using resilient strength in the blocking arm and of keeping your knees relaxed and your weight low.

Try using both sides of your body, then change roles and you be the attacker while your partner tries out some blocks. Be observant and notice what works and what does not.

In reality, no attack will happen in the neat, tidy and classical manner which you are practising now. You are practising these pre-arranged movements in order to programme into your body the *type* of movement – strongly based and with powerful momentum, which will help you to fend off a blow. It will then be available to you in whatever form you need it as and when that happens. You are helping your body to avoid panic reactions like the one below, which might make it difficult for you to look after yourself (see Figure 13).

Figure 13

You are helping it instead to internalize reactions like the automatic adoption of the sideways-on stance, which gives you many more options (see Figure 14, p. 50).

Escapes

Let us now turn to escapes – how to free yourself from an unwelcome grip or restraint. Once again, no attacker will grab you in a neat, tidy, and predictable manner, but, by practising manœuvres like these, you will be habituating your body to key principles that will help you effect a spontaneous and powerful release from any grip that you do not want to be held in.

Figure 14

Single wrist release

Ask your partner to hold your wrist – same side to same side (i.e. your left wrist in his/her right wrist).

If you try to escape by pulling away backwards, the grip and determination is simply strengthened – try it and see.

When held against your will, always ask yourself: where is the exit from this? Logically speaking, what is the way out? And then do not waste your time and energy struggling to get out in an impossible direction.

Look at your partner's grip on your wrist. You cannot get out

50

through the curved, solid palm of their hand, you have got to get out through the grip between thumb and fingers.

The way to get out is to move *towards* the attacker rather than away from them, to lay your forearm against his/her forearm so that you are moving as though to go back to back with him/her. Twist your wrist away and down – with a yell if you want to! The leverage of your arm against the attacker's effects a joint lock on his/her elbow. The twisting and downwards movement, and the unexpected moving in rather than away, can snap you out of the strongest grip.

Your knees relaxed and your centre of gravity in your hips are essentials for this technique.

Practise with your partner. Use both arms and take both roles and become familiar with what works for you. It is important, too, to feel how powerful the releasing action is.

Diagonal wrist release

This release also relies on an unexpected inwards movement, and a twist.

Ask your partner to grip your right wrist in his/her left. Once again pull back and see what happens: you will find that the grip simply tightens. Open your hand and move towards your 'attacker' (see Figure 15).
Wind your open hand under his/her and reach over onto the top of the forearm. This creates leverage of your wrist against attackers and breaks you out through the exit which is the gap between fingers and thumbs.

Push firmly, with your resilient strength, down onto the attacker's arm and his/her grip will release. If it feels useful, grasp your attacker's arm and twist it firmly round behind his/her back, pulling it up between the shoulder blades. Push firmly so that he/she staggers away.

This sequence feels very elaborate at first. Go through it several times in slow motion, and when it begins to feel familiar, speed it up and begin to bring some power into it.

If your everyday life does not include learning sequences of physical movement it takes some time to stop feeling as though the physical

Figure 15

logic will forever elude you. Try not to collapse into feelings of physical illiteracy. It takes a little time, that is all.

Double wrist releases

A. Ask your partner to hold you by both wrists. Once again, check that if you pull away, you will reinforce the attacker's grip and control of you. Try it. Now look down and ask yourself where the exit is: it is of course through the gaps between your attacker's fingers and thumbs.

Relax your knees, centre yourself in your hips, and flood your torso and arms with resilient power.

Twist your wrists sharply in and down. You may escape at this point. Yell with the twist if you want to! If you did not get out, twist sharply up and out and this will probably release you. If not, continue with another downward twist and another upward one. If you still are not out, wait and see what happens next. Look at p. 69 'What if it doesn't work?'

If you escape on an upward twist, a useful counter-attack can be to continue the upward momentum of your hands, grab your attacker's head, pull it downwards and simultaneously raise your knee. His/her face will crash uncomfortably down onto your knee.

Practise with your partner, as always emphasizing good, relaxed, powerful stance, and resilient, rather than tense strength.

If you practise pulling the attacker's head down onto your knee *be extremely careful* to control the manœuvre as it is easy accidentally to make contact when you did not intend to.

Start slowly and gradually increase in speed and power. Take both roles because this gives you valuable insights into what works well and why.

B. If an attacker has large hands, he or she may be able to hold both your hands in one of his/her, creating the alarming situation where your attacker has a hand free while both of yours are confined.

You may be able to escape by relaxing, dropping your hands a couple of inches, and then exploding up. Your hands are then close to your attacker's face for any counter-attack you feel is useful. As well as the counter-attacks already mentioned, do not forget that you can curve your hands like the claws of a big cat and scratch determinedly downward with them. You will leave tracks on your attacker which may be useful for identifying him or her afterwards. A claw counter-attack is useful to follow up a release which threw your hands in an upward momentum. The downward clawing movement follows on naturally.

If you are unable to escape by this drop-down explode-up sequence, try utilizing the strength of the attacker's grip. Pull your attacker towards you and deliver a sharp kick or knee strike to the testicles if the attacker is male, or a stamping kick down through her knee (if you are wearing hard shoes or high heels, scrape your shoe edge or heel down the front of her calf and stamp down on the top of her foot too), or if your legs are supple enough for you to do so comfortably, execute a powerful pushing kick to the lower abdomen.

Walk through A and B with your partner and become familiar with how to escape from both types of double wrist grips. Increase in speed and power when you are ready, and do not forget to change roles so that you both experience each side of this technique.

Front strangle release

A strangle hold around the neck is a very serious attack: you have only a short time to neutralize it. If you are reading with interest but not actually practising any techniques, do take time to practise these ones. More people are murdered by strangulation than by any other kind of attack, except for battering with a blunt instrument. You need to know what to do about it.

- Protect your airway
- Strong counter-attack
- Escape

Protect your airway It is horrifying to be grasped around the throat. It may take a moment to assimilate what is happening. When you do realize, you may react by throwing your head back to take a gulp of air. We need to learn and internalize a different reflex: that is, to *draw the chin in sharply to protect the airway*. It takes less than two minutes complete compression of your airway to cause you to black out. Once you have blacked out there is no more you can do to protect yourself. Simply remembering to draw your chin in rather than to tilt your head back if attacked around the throat, might save your life. So long as you are able to get oxygen into your body you have the power to think and move. So long as you can think and move, you can go on fighting to free yourself.

Protect your airway!

Strong counter-attack In the case of someone making as dangerous an attack on you as this you may well feel you want to make a strong counter-attack in order to immobilize your attacker for some minutes while you escape.

Tiger-mouth-hand The best counter-attack is tiger-mouth-hand, which we learned on p. 38.

> Draw your chin in to protect your airway, then step sharply in and do tiger-mouth-hand counter-attack to the throat, *with complete commitment.*

Your attacker is doing something which could deprive you of your life. Do not hesitate to make this powerful response to save yourself. You have every right. Your attacker will cough violently and become very uncomfortable. While s/he concentrates on getting her/his breath back, you rush away.

If tiger-mouth-hand is not possible because, for example, your attacker has long arms and has locked them at the elbows, or you tried it and missed, or are prevented from using it for any other reason, there are alternatives.

Upper arm pinch If your attacker is in shirt sleeves:

> You can pinch and twist sharply a little flesh under each of their upper arms. It is surprisingly painful, like a wasp sting, and normally causes a person to react to it – and therefore in this case to loosen or remove the grip around your throat.

Try it out on your partner and let them try it out on you. It will make you jump!

Elbow joint counter-attack Draw your chin in. Hold your attacker's left upper arm in your left hand. Centre your strength. Smash the palm of your right hand onto the back of his/her elbow. Extend your resilient power *through* the elbow with the blow. This will certainly hurt and may well break the elbow – either way your attacker will tend to release the grip from your throat to rub and examine the hurt elbow. This is your opportunity to escape. Go!

Practise the manœuvre with your partner, but only slowly. On no account try it out with full power: you will hurt one another. Simply learn and become familiar with the movement, and add it to your repertoire.

Arm weave Draw your chin in. Thread your stronger arm

over one of the the attacker's arms and lever up his/her other arm. With your other hand, push up strongly under the attacker's elbow to release his grip (see Figure 16). Finish with a side punch to the face. Again practise this slowly together with your partner, and change roles.

Figure 16

Explode up Draw your chin in. Draw your arms down to your waist then shoot your arms up between your attacker's arms and twist sharply out, knocking his/her arms away. Finish with a side punch to the face, or pull his/her face down onto your bent knee.

Practise slowly with your partner, and gradually increase speed and power. Be careful with the face-to-knee manœuvre. Each try out each role.

Grip and twist testicles If your attacker is male and you can reach the genital area then grip and twist his testicles. As we have already said, this will cause intense pain, and to all intents and purposes your attacker will have to concentrate his attention entirely on himself for several minutes. You escape at this point.

Practise with your partner, making a clear and decisive manœuvre.

Become familiar with this range of responses to a front strangle attack. One of them will probably become your 'favourite', and that one will probably work best for you.

Escape When you have effected a successful release and counter-attack, continue to use your resilient strength and your determination to get away. Certainly your legs may be shaking, certainly you may be in shock, but keep moving and keep active to achieve this last part of the technique. Think of doing whatever you choose in the way of sport and exercise to ensure that your stamina and strength are in good shape, but rest assured that your body will do what you need it to in circumstances like these:

> To all of you who ever wondered how you could run in a threatening situation without the proper footwear, as I had often wondered, I'll tell you – it's a cinch. I ran bare-foot . . . and never noticed that my feet were barefoot and cut and bleeding slightly until much later when it was pointed out to me.
> Jane Polansky, 'A Woman of Common Sense and Courage' from *Her Wits About Her* ed. Caignon and Groves, The Women's Press

Rear strangle release

Rear strangle holds are also very alarming, with the added fear caused by the fact that you cannot see your attacker. Remember that fear is your friend, it is what your body does to increase your chances of survival by making more strength, breath and speed of reaction available to you. Learn to use the energy given to you by your fear, and you will not become paralysed. Get hold of your down-to-earth determination not to let any attacker manipulate you through fear. With a rear strangle attack you have exactly the same priorities as with a front one:

- Protect your airway
- Strong counter-attack
- Escape

Protect your airway Protect your airway by turning your head and tucking your chin into the crook of your attacker's elbow, thus preventing him/her from compressing your airway with the full force of the forearm.

Strong counter-attack and escape *Downward twist* Moving your feet and hips, wriggle around until you disturb your partner's stance and his/her balance shifts and he/she has to move his/her feet.

You will feel the grip loosen and you may be able to escape straight away. If you cannot get completely away you will probably be able to shift yourself so that your head is being held by your attacker beside his/her waist rather than against the chest. Once here, you can reach behind your attacker and grip and twist his testicles, or putting your near arm around the attacker's waist, punch up strongly into the abdomen with your outside arm (see Figure 17).

Figure 17

Practise the sequence with your partner, building up speed and momentum as you improve. Both take each roles in turn to develop your skills and insights.

Little finger joint lock Tuck your chin into the crook of your attacker's elbow. Prise the little finger of the strangling arm hand out and bend it back as far as you can with your fingers while pushing its joint forwards with your thumb. Most people find this agonizingly uncomfortable and need to withdraw the hand straight away – thus letting go of you. You may well be able to extricate yourself from a rear strangle hold simply by this joint lock. Try it out with your partner, controlling the pressure carefully.

Back elbow strike and backward stamp You may want or need to try some backwards strikes in order to unsettle or loosen the attacker's grip or simply to continue to assert yourself before you have a repeat go at a joint lock or a downward twist escape.

Your elbow is a marvellous body weapon. In this kind of attack you can slam it firmly back into your attacker's abdomen. Even if he/she steps back to avoid your elbow, you have taken his/her concentration and determination away from the dangerous grip on your throat. If you manage to make contact then so much the better.

You can stamp firmly back onto your attacker's feet, or kick back to the knee and scrape the outside of your foot, or your high heel, if you are wearing one, down the front of the leg. This will disturb your attacker's balance, and if you make good contact will cause pain and distraction sufficient for your attacker to loosen his/her grip.

Try the strike and the stamp out with your partner, controlling the impact for practice purposes. If you use them for real, remember the principle of striking *through* the target.

Release from backward grab If you are grabbed and held from behind, use a downward twist or go heavy to elude the grip.

Downward twist A corkscrew downwards wriggle will help you evade a bear hug applied from behind, as will the young children's expedient of 'going heavy' when they do not want to be moved.

Anyone who has tried to propel a reluctant child upstairs to bed or cram a recalcitrant toddler into a pushchair will know how difficult it is to move anyone who does not want to be moved.

Get in touch with the stubborn, lumpish child in yourself to make your whole body heavy and difficult to handle. Get your partner to grab you from behind in any way he/she likes – apart from a rear strangle – and try out both a downward twisting movement, and making your body very heavy and awkward, to disrupt his or her grip and ability to control you physically.

After you have tried both, change roles and see how it goes the other way around. Take some time when you have both tried both methods to discuss how it felt.

Add these techniques of blocks and releases to your repertoire of counter-attacks, and you now have the beginnings of a working armoury of personal safety skills.

Surviving if you fall

We have a real terror of falling to the ground and being brutally kicked. This is not a stupid terror because hundreds of people are damaged this way in vicious attacks every year.

However, we can become less afraid and more powerful if we become aware of how to:

- Fall well
- Be mobile on the ground
- Go on fighting on the ground

Falling well

Falling without hurting yourself is a valuable skill in both physical and emotional terms. It is a new skill for many of us in the West who feel we must be either up *or* down. The way of the martial arts which is based on Buddhism and the Tao lets us know that we are both up *and* down, yin *and* yang, dark *and* light. Being up is only part of the next movement down. Being down is only part of being on your way up.

If you really want to comprehend this in your body and your heart, study aikido.

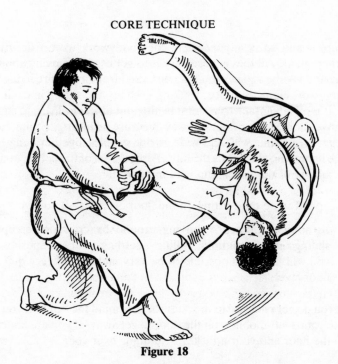

Figure 18

The wonderful circular whirling throws and falls of aikido show up-energy transforming into down-energy, and falling down turning into rising up, quite perfectly (see Figure 18).

For the purposes here, of extending our safety skills, we need to learn to fall into the floor, curling into it rather than crashing or colliding anxiously with it. From my disreputable youth I remember falling off a bicycle in Cambridge while drunk. The road floated up and gently wrapped itself along my body. I was not hurt at all. Of course this was a stupid way to behave and it was luck I did not deserve which caused it to end safely and not tragically. It has however provided me with an image of how to fall gently without hurting myself.

Try tumbling – backwards, forwards, and to the sides – onto big cushions or mats until you are used to it, then onto the hard floor. Curve and roll as you meet the surface you are falling onto, let it and not you absorb the energy of your fall.

How to be mobile on the ground

Anyone who works or lives with young children is at an advantage here – and so is anyone who does bodywork with a floorwork component. All that is necessary is to get used to moving about at ground level – a place you may be exiled from if you are living in a city, working in an office, walking in shoes and sitting in chairs.

It is an advantage to general health and fitness to learn to sit and move more on the floor anyway, because squatting, sitting cross-legged, or sitting with legs wide astride or soles together, lengthens the hamstring and opens the hips. Also, the set of the pelvis, and the flexibility of the lower spine are improved.

Spend some time sitting on the floor every day if you can.

In addition, practise moving around by crawling, creeping, sliding on your tummy, rolling, scuttling, and scampering. As you will find, it is possible to be very mobile and very quick at floor level.

If you do get knocked to the floor, bear in mind the fact that you can use your swift mobility on the floor to get away. If you are knocked to the floor and your attacker is standing over you:

Do not curl up into a ball. This only protects the soft surface of your abdomen, it does not protect your spine, your kidneys, your neck, or your head.

Instead, support yourself on your elbows, swivel round to face the attacker, and extend your less favourite leg towards them, pulling your strong leg, knee in towards your chest. It is pulled in so that it is holding all the potential energy, and can spring forwards when you need it to. Keep moving around if the attacker does, and keep your straight leg pointing towards them. If he/she begins to move towards you, gather your awareness and focus into your strong leg. If he/she then moves into range, either explode the straight leg out to stamp onto his/her knee, or explode out your straight leg and bring it up sharply between your attackers legs, attacking the testicles or groin. As soon as you have impacted on the attacker so that his/her attention is refocused onto him-/herself, roll over onto your feet and run away.

When you are in any struggle where you are underneath or below your attacker, you are closer to some of the body targets, than if you were both standing. Bear this advantage in mind.

How to go on fighting on the ground

Floor pins

You may get caught in a floor pin.

If someone is sitting on your abdomen as you lie on your back, and is pinning you down by the wrists, do not waste your energy struggling ineffectually. This is one occasion where perhaps what you need to do initially is to wait:

If you want to try to free your hands, try, with resilient strength, to shoot them up along the floor and then out down in wide arcs. If that does not work, then wait.

Before your attacker does anything else, such as moving his or her hands to your throat, or moving to make a sexual assault, he/she will have to release your wrists, and you will also feel a shift of balance in his/her body weight. In that time you will be able to snatch your hands away and this would be a good time to yell. Thrust your hips up and twist them sharply to further upset your attacker's balance – you may be able to throw them off you completely in this manœuvre. Whether you unseat them completely or not, follow up with a hard counter-attack – punch to the groin or grip and twist the testicles, pinch and twist flesh on the inner thigh, or if your attacker's face is within more convenient range, direct an effective counter-attack to their face, such that his/her attention is drawn to him-/herself and away from you, and you can get away. The principle in a floor pin is to remember that your hips are the most powerful part of you for unsettling your attacker's balance, and that your attacker has several vulnerable body targets within your reach once your hands are free. You may have to keep your cool while you wait for a moment when you can be effective rather than wasting your energy.

If you are pinned to the floor by someone sitting astride your back, the principles are the same: your hips are where your greatest pivotal strength is, and your hands can reach a number of your attacker's body targets, once they are free.

Pull your knees up under you as much as possible to make less effective any attempts to smash your face down into the ground. Concentrate on strong whole-body twisting movements of the hips to get your upper body round to where your hands can start to be effective, and to unsettle the balance of your attacker as much as possible.

Practise floor pins with your partner, working on them slowly at first, then gradually building up speed and power. When you feel ready to do so you may want to practise with heavier partners, to begin to get a sense of what it is like to shift around and control the body weight of somebody much heavier than yourself. If so, be careful always to choose partners who are interested in working constructively with you. Centre your strength in your hips and surge all movements out from there.

Understanding group attacks

A group attack is a particularly horrifying experience, although perhaps less common than we fear. Less than 1 per cent of assaults are committed by multiple attackers, and assaults in total constitute only 6 per cent of reported crime. Nevertheless, it is important to have a sense of how to cope, how to remain powerful, if such an event should happen in your life.

There are two points of principle in coping with group attacks:

- Treat the group as a single energy source
- Identify the leader and act against him/her

A group is pivotal around the charisma of one person, and so is really a single energy source. If the group members act effectively at all, they are going to act together; if their energy is scattered they are far less dangerous and easier to evade. See the group as something like a swarm – which only really has one kind of momentum.

Identifying the leader is usually relatively straightforward. Watch the body language – who are the others glancing at for a lead, or to check whether what they are doing is alright? This person is the leader. His or her own body language will be more swaggering and open than other group members. This is your target person and you need to address yourself to him/her and direct an effective counter-attack towards him/her as soon as possible. If you can make an effective counter-attack on the leader and then run you have the advantage of stretching out the group energy by creating a situation where you string them out in a line running after you.

If you are restrained by two people it is possible to use what you already know to do an effective double release.

Double release

If you are held by both arms you begin to escape by upsetting the rhythm of the people restraining you (see Figure 19).

Figure 19

With your *weaker* leg take a lunging step forwards then a lunging step back. This leaves your strong leg ready to come up.

On the step back with your weaker leg, turn your whole body, using hip strength, in the direction of that leg. Bring the strong-leg knee sharply up into the attacker's groin in front, then stamp back to the attacker behind your foot, following this by swinging your foot up between his/her legs. Your front-on attacker will have doubled forwards in reaction to your knee attack to the groin. Push your open hand hard into his/her face and drag the curved fingers downwards, hooking into the eyes as you go. You should then have caused enough pain to both of them for them to take their attention to themselves, and let you go.

An alternative would be:

Double-release (2)

Restrained by a person on each side:

> Turn with full body strength, (not just arm strength) to the right and stamp down on this attacker's knee with your right foot. Turn 180° frontwards and stamp down on the other attacker's knee with your right foot. (If you are left-footed do both strikes with your left foot.) A determined stamp *through* the attacker's legs will cause enough pain for them to loosen their grip on you at least momentarily – and momentarily is all you need to start running.

As with all the other techniques we are discussing, a double restraint is unlikely to happen in a neat and tidy fashion. Practise the techniques we have described here, because this will help your body to internalize good basic principle responses. The keys are:

- Use whole-body strength
- Make decisive counter-attacks to good targets – face, throat, groin, or knee
- Stay in touch with your will and determination to survive and escape

Understanding weapon attacks

The whole subject of attacks and self-defence around edged weapons is fraught. Once you realize how small a hole in the human body can be to be fatal – one inch penetration in the spine between the shoulder blades; one inch in the area below the breast bone where so many major organs lie close to the surface of the body; half-an-inch in the area of the carotid or femoral arteries – you are suddenly aware of the softness, the fragility, the vulnerability of the human body; that there are tubes and membranes conducting and containing the materials within you without which your life quickly leaks away. This realization is a paradoxical thing: it is essentially humane and humanizing, and reminds us how tenuous our position in the universe really is. However, the insight is a scaring one, and for purposes of staying safe we have to channel our fear into energy, into accuracy and determination, into knowing which parts of ourselves we need to keep particularly safe from edged weapons and into knowing how to resist danger.

It is heartening to know that in the USA, 57 per cent of women threatened with rape at knife-point resisted and were neither raped nor cut. Co-operating with a rapist or attacker who threatens you with a knife is no guarantee of your eventual survival. When you judge the moment is right, you have little to lose from a coherent attempt to get away. Stay strongly connected with your own will and determination.

Making the knife or edged-weapon harmless

A first line of defence is sometimes possible because many attackers with knives are very tense and very focused on the knife itself, having little peripheral vision working well.

Throw something over the knife or over your attacker's head to cover his eyes: throw liquid from a drink or a vase of flowers into his eyes; impale a heavy briefcase or handbag onto the knife. This will disarm the attacker for the crucial number of seconds it will take you to begin your escape.

Bear this principle in mind: that if you can get something heavy stuck onto the knife or get a heavy jacket for example thrown over it or them, you are making things very much easier for yourself; and it may be all you need to do to resolve the situation.

Controlling the knife

This may not be possible, and you may have to control the knife/scissors/screwdriver – all edged household objects are potentially lethal weapons and must be noticed as such if ever there is an intruder in your house. Never, ever leave such objects lying around in your house where they could be picked up during, for example, an interrupted burglary, and used against you.

Most attackers will use an edged weapon in their forward hand.

Think of the knife simply as an extension of the arm. If you can control the arm, you can control the weapon (see Figure 20).

First of all, and absolutely essentially, get into a sideways stance. This turns your major body targets away from the knife. The best blocking position is as in the illustration, but notice especially that the forward blocking hand is turned palm-inwards. This is vital because it turns the major wrist arteries away from the blade. The rear hand, again palm in, covers as much as possible of the soft abdominal front.

Figure 20

If you have to fight in an edged weapon attack, expect to be cut.

Do not drop the guard from your vital body organs because you are cut on the forward hand and forearm and see some blood.

You can cope with quite a number of cuts on the outside of your forearm without losing too much blood – and that is why you have put it there.

If your attacker then moves in:

Use that forward hand to deflect the wrist – step aside as you do, and push hard forwards and down on the back of his/her elbow. Crash down hard onto the elbow with an elbow attack or a stamp down kick depending how far down you have brought the attacker. This strong blow to the elbow will sprain or break it and will release the grip. Kick the knife well away. In such a dangerous situation you may well also want to make a final counter-attack to further immobilize your attacker, such as a strong kick to the face or a punch down to the throat or neck. However, only do so if it feels safe, or vitally important, to take those extra seconds. Your main priority is to get completely away.

If the edged weapon is in the attacker's rear hand this is a very much more dangerous situation and suggests that the person has used edged weapons before.

As far as possible, stay completely out of range. Keep the same guard as before, always remembering, palms inwards to keep the major wrist arteries away from the weapon. However, your only really effective option here is to stop the attacker by attacking his knee as he approaches. Do not look away. Stamp down *hard* on the approaching knee. Remember it only takes 15 lbs of pressure to break a knee, and you have a potential of 100 lbs of pressure in a strong, adult kick. Use that pressure well if you find yourself in this predicament and it can save your life.

What if it doesn't work?

If you work hard on this core competence stage of the book, you will become increasingly adept at using the techniques. You will also, however, without doubt, often find yourself asking 'What if it doesn't work?'

Let us start by untangling this question a bit; part of it may be 'What if my attacker is better trained in fighting than me?'

First, it should be out-of-the-question that any person who is properly trained in martial arts would attack you. Responsible martial arts clubs sift through who they train and continually emphasize that techniques are never to be used outside the club except in last-resort self-defence. The vast majority of properly trained martial artists, therefore, will not provoke or collude with trouble in any way and will always choose to walk or run away from it wherever possible. It would be entirely against everything they have been taught to use their knowledge in making an assault. Nevertheless, it has to be acknowledged that a number of people may have been trained in unarmed combat in disreputable clubs where they have not been given the necessary philosophical background to go with their techniques, and that some martial

artists may have 'gone off the rails' in terms of use of alcohol- or
drug-abuse, or loss of emotional control. It is also true that there is
evidence of men practising aggressive fighting techniques in prison,
of learning unarmed combat methods in other situations, and of
being aggressive and knowledgeable physically simply as a result of
having grown up in tough environments.

Second, you can cope with this 'What if. . . ?' by acknowledging
it. Although it is unlikely, it is possible that your attacker may know
some special techniques. Your answer to this is to be angry,
determined, and unimpressed. As long as you are still breathing and
conscious, you can fight back with power, using your own knowledge of body targets and the key principles of the core technique, to
work for your own survival. Use your voice too. Let your emotion
about someone using trained technique for purposes of violent
assault be not terror but utter contempt.

Another 'What if. . . ?' is 'What if I try something and get it
wrong?' If you feel you are someone who often gets things 'wrong',
you may worry that you will be just plain incompetent in fighting
back. But be assured that fighting back is what your organism wants
you to do – so let it make you! Once you are clear about your core
techniques they – or adaptations of them – will come to you when
you need them. If you try something and it doesn't have the desired
effect, don't feed it into your 'I'm no good' script and become
passive; do something else!

. . . I felt a nauseous inability or unwillingness to knee him in the
crotch, though I did jab once at his Adam's apple, but the blow
glanced off in a rubbery manner, and the man looked disgusted.
He cocked his head to one side in what I guess he thought was a
cunning pose, and said: 'I'll get you down, if you don't give me
muh glasses'. 'Here's your glasses', I said rapidly, and as he took
them with his free hands, I wound up and jabbed him in the eyes
with stiff fingertips, still with no conscious plan and with all my
weight in back of it. I felt the blow land true, not as impact alone,
but as a shock from my fingers all up my arm. I thought of the
man's senses crashing back in from pain. As he fell back with a
grunt and released my arm, I ran . . .
Pat Deer. 'I let him have it right in the eyes' from *Her Wits about
Her* ed. Caignon and Groves, The Women's Press

As you work with your partner other 'What if. . . ?s' will come into your mind: 'What if an attacker got into my car?' 'What if an attacker held my arm back in this way?' 'What if someone jumped me from behind if I was sitting in a chair?' 'What if. . . ?'

Working through the 'What if's. . . ?' is a most valuable part of your development. Act them out together, slow them down to slow motion, and work out what your options are, what you think you could do. Try different responses out. This work really helps you to be adaptable and flexible in your technique and to get away from the feeling 'I don't know this one, there's nothing I can do, I don't know how to deal with it'.

Spend plenty of time working out your 'What if's. . . ?' and you will feel not depowered but empowered by the process.

3
Attitude

Figure 21

So far in this book we have looked at how to establish a foundation of inner peace, followed by a collection of strong effective core techniques which can be thoroughly absorbed into your physical body as skills you can call upon any time.

The third component we are about to add is *attitude*. Everybody knows from seeing the survivors of the playground bully, the survivors in office politics, and the survivors of marital betrayals or tragedy and bereavement, that attitude is enormously important in one's ability to get through an unpleasant situation and come out the other side. Any individual's 'attitude' is made up of a complex mixture of qualities and issues covering the way you feel about yourself and the way you interact with the people around you and the environment itself. We will separate some of these issues out and look at them one at a time. With some of them there are awareness exercises which you can do with a partner. Exactly the same thinking applies in your choice of partner as you used for choosing a partner in the physical exercises. Be sure to choose someone who will work mutually with you.

Dress

The way in which we dress is one of the primary forms of non-verbal communication we have with the world. Whatever you wear makes a statement of some sort. Even if, as I certainly did for one part of my life, you try to pay no attention whatsoever to what you wear, and literally wear 'any old thing', that in itself becomes a statement which is made by you and can be read by others. Your choice of clothes signals your income bracket, your sense of where you 'fit in' in the world, and the signals you want to give other people about your profession, your feelings of self-worth or otherwise, and your membership or alliance with any sub-group – banker, skinhead, Greenpeace, artistic, business-like, homely, bohemian, heterosexual, homosexual, self-sufficient, athletic, sensual, respectable, imaginative, and so on.

You may, on reflection, notice that you work hard to look recognizably part of your sub-culture, or to look entirely separate; you may notice that you look exceptional wherever you are or that you tend to blend in wherever you are. Take some time to talk with your partner about how you dress in this present part of your life, and how you feel about it.

Notice anything which, on reflection, surprises you, and anything which you would like to change. Notice anything you feel pleased about. If you do not feel pleased about anything, do not get bogged down in negative feelings, but have some time with the support of your partner to think over what gets in your way, and why.

Dressing in a way which feels expressive of what we really want of ourselves, feels powerful, and is good in itself. It also contributes to personal safety in the very real sense of increasing our sense of self-worth.

However, let us look at the particular issues of dress that may have a direct bearing on your personal safety.

Free or restrictive?

Do you wear clothes that are tight or loose? Do they restrict your movement at the knees, groin, hips, or under-arm? Do you ever wear anything that is so tight that it hurts, or so restrictive that you have to make odd movements to get in and out of cars, on and off transport, up and down steps and stairs? Do you sometimes wear a smaller size than is comfortable because it upsets you to have a larger size number on your clothes label? These questions are important for both men and women. If your answer to one or more of them feels to you to be unreasonable or different from what you would like, do not label yourself guilty or stupid. Instead, take the time to take in the observation you have made, and to notice any changes you would like to make. Any changes you do make, you will do in your own time – but do allow yourself to notice if you literally 'tie yourself up' in your own clothes and make it more difficult to keep yourself safe because they limit your potential range of movement.

Also, allow yourself to notice whether you ever wear clothes that hurt you. Women and men frequently do so without ever thinking it over, and thinking over why. Maybe, on reflection, you might want to choose not to.

Personal style is a subtle and powerful mix of self-expression, social norms, and other matters like time and money. Nonetheless, it is a simple fact that a person who wears clothes in which they can breathe and move freely looks dynamic, mobile, and strong, and can use core safety techniques without impediment.

Shoes, hair, and ornaments

Women and men are probably safest in the footwear which they wear most often, since they are able to run and manoeuvre best in whatever their feet are most accustomed to. If you regularly wear high heels you will be quite capable of running, turning, and twisting in them; if you wear loose sandals, or heavy boots, or soft trainers, or city courts, most of the time, you will be pretty quick off the mark in them. You will *not* be so fast or so stable in shoes you wear much less often. If, for example, you only wear high heels on rare evenings out, consider choosing a style which you can easily kick off if you need to make a quick getaway. On any other occasion that you have to wear unfamiliar footwear, be aware that the muscles of your feet, hips, and back, are not aligned to cope with it, and raise your awareness of any risks you are running anywhere that you go.

It is interesting to become increasingly aware of the quality of the contact between your feet and the ground. The more bodywork you do, and body awareness of any kind, the more you will become aware of things like the fact that your feet have carried you around for every year of your life (except the first one) and so how valuable they are to you. They become more articulate and expressive, more like hands. It is quite different having the whole footprint on the ground as opposed to just the small portions of the heel and the ball of the foot on which you can only balance. For your safety and personal power, take care to notice what sort of shoes and what sort of contact with the earth feel best.

The safety point with hair is essentially one of vision. Does your hair regularly fall down into your eyes and restrict your vision? If it does, it is a risk when if you find yourself in danger you may have problems taking in everything you need to visually.

Ornaments such as earrings, necklaces, handbags, bracelets and so forth, are an identifiable risk if they do not detach or snap immediately when pulled. Anything which holds when pulled and which you cannot easily slip out of can be used to pull you along or pull you over with. Be aware particularly of choosing earrings which will pull right out if yanked: and if you are in a situation where you feel the atmosphere is rapidly deteriorating or becoming threatening, you may want quietly to remove your earrings or other jewellery by which you could be pushed, pulled, controlled or hurt.

A last important point concerns personal headphones. If you tend to walk around with a Walkman on, remember that you are cutting out a very important sense – your hearing – which can warn you of a hostile approach.

Provocative?

This question is controversial and problematic. Rape trials have been brutally complicated for years by judges, lawyers, and the innate sexism of our culture, with savage and detailed commentary on the *victim's* clothing as being a powerful part of the defence case. In no other crime is so much energy used in proving the victim guilty rather than proving the defendant innocent! A regular part of this harassment of the victim is to suggest that her choice of clothing was a contributory factor in the attack. Countless rape survivors have, in addition to all the other aspects of the aftermath of the rape they have had to deal with, had long-lasting anxiety about their choice of clothes:

> . . . my life has been changed in ways I would never have thought possible, including problems with sex, walking alone, trying to decide if the clothes I wear will stand up in court if I'm attacked again and have to testify to my good faith.

'A Woman of Common Sense and Courage' from *Her Wits About Her* ed. Caignon and Groves, The Women's Press

This is one of the bitterest double binds that our culture puts its women into. Millions of words and images, daily, directly and indirectly leave every single woman in the country in no doubt that a major part of her life-project is to be as sexually attractive as possible. She should slim, she should exercise, she should inform herself of fashion trends and invest a large proportion of her income in whatever approximation of them she can afford; she should try to appear younger than she really is, laugh, prance, and if she must have opinions of her own, express them tactfully; she should mess around with 'lingerie', make-up and perfumes, otherwise she is not making the proper effort with herself; if she is too heavy, or too old, or too individualistic to engage in this project, she is marginalized, ridiculed, or ignored.

But – if that woman is attacked, indecently assaulted, or raped, she will find that her efforts to be as sexually attractive as possible – efforts that, to some extent every other woman in the population is making too – will be counted as proofs that her character is devious, promiscuous, and inviting of rape.

What are women, and men, to do about this double bind? We need short-term and long-term responses to the crisis.

Long-term, the discussion of sex and sexuality, sense and sensuality, power and gender, has to struggle on. We have to think about what our children see, hear, and believe about sexuality. We have to find the strength to sell our own truths in the area and to challenge things that we feel are damaging and abusive. We have to listen, share, and develop a sexual awareness that does not inevitably lead to the blurring of sex and power where assault and attack on vulnerable individuals is fuelled by the way sex is described in the culture itself.

Short-term, there is a real question about whether you, today, this week, this month, want to adjust the way you dress in order to be more safe. The 'Reclaim the Night' marches of the 1980s asserted:

> However we dress, wherever we go
> Yes means yes, and no means no!

You may feel quite unwilling to compromise at all on this

principle. It is a choice you are entitled to make. You may, on the other hand, feel that for the time being this is not a safe environment in which to wear in public clothing which is linked, by the pornographic industry, in the culture's collective unconscious, with direct and general sexual invitation.

This is miserable but necessary material to contemplate. Talk about it with supportive and interested friends and partners. Do not allow yourself to be doubly hurt by anyone ridiculing your concern. Women and men will continue to be hurt by sexist conditioning until we can understand it well enough to change it.

There is of course a second important sense of the word 'provoc ative' to consider, and that is, whether the clothing you choose is likely to provoke *anger*.

Wearing manifestly expensive designer clothing in a poor ghetto area might be an implicitly insulting and provocative thing to do. Wearing the football colours of one team in an area considered to be the territory of another, would, in many places in the UK, be seen to be extremely provocative. Wearing clothing or insignia clearly identified with one cultural or religious group in places mainly frequented by rival groups, might well provoke anger.

Pluralism, tolerance and creative interaction, is surely what we should all aim for in the end, but centuries of cross-cultural, inter-religious and gang violence in our cities makes it clear that such a hope is a long-term and not a short-term objective.

There may be times when it feels important to you not to adapt or adjust what you wear in order not to provoke anger. If I was close to a National Front rally being held in London now, I would be disinclined in the first instance to avoid wearing badges or T-shirts which marked me out as a liberal. However, if I lived for years in a repressive fascist regime, wearing the same badges and T-shirts would be a much more risky act and would involve a different kind of decision.

The safety point is this: it makes sense to be aware of any provocation your clothing may cause among the people around you. Make your choices on the basis of a realistic assessment of the risk, balanced with your own need for integrity. Be clear that it feels like a definite and positive choice for you. If circumstances change, or if you change, be prepared to allow yourself to change your choice too.

Well-being

The general state that our bodies are in gives a pretty clear indication of the value that we place upon ourselves. We may have developed our intellects assiduously and yet somehow lost touch with our bodies, or become fit in specific ways which may not leave us strong and supple all over. We may eat irregularly, or unhealthily, or far too much, or far too little, and we may be in the grip of various addictions.

It is in fact pretty difficult to be well in a polluted and tense world, but it is an important part of our safety strategy to think about what kind of condition our bodies are in now, how we would like them to be, and how to travel across the gap in between.

We could think about these issues one at a time.

Food and nutrition

Anyone who has actually tried to eat correctly over the last decade or two will be completely bemused by now by volte-face after volte-face about the benefits and dangers of eggs, milk, cheese, meat, fish, fruit, fibre, vegetables, spring water, sugar, honey, and just about every food group you can think of. Each has been approved and disapproved of, and the percentage of our diet each should take up has been adjusted and re-adjusted over and over again. Add to this the problems of pesticides and fertilizers on fruit and vegetables, the pollution which fish absorb from the sea, and the hormones and antibiotics with which most animals reared for slaughter have been treated, and the problem of a fresh, balanced diet, starts to seem to be an insoluble one.

All we can do is try to notice what the balance in our own eating is, and if we feel heavy, or tired, or sluggish, to consider that an adjustment in that balance might be worth trying. A moderate and non-obsessive approach would be best, if that is possible in our hyped and confused culture. We do need to consider the quality and balance of what we eat as part of maintaining our bodies in a state that they can stay safe.

The quantity eaten is important too. Over- and under-eating can happen for many reasons to women and to men. Caught in an endless pursuit of thinness, many women and some men become acutely conscious of everything they take into their bodies as food, feeling that though they desire it, it is a dangerous substance that will make them lose their urgent battle with the scales. You may undereat during the day because the stress of your work churns your stomach into a state of continual acidity so that you cannot face food, then gorge uncomfortably at night because you arrive home famished. You may feel sensorially deprived or bored and unfulfilled and eat too much because it is only food which, at the present time, gives you satisfaction and pleasure. Giving and receiving large meals might be a way in which business is done in your profession. In your peer group there may be much discussion of weight and size, with power points being gained for becoming thinner and lost for growing heavier. The frightening eating disorders of anorexia nevosa and anorexia bulimia bear out the extremes to which eating and non-eating can become distorted in a culture which has great difficulty in sorting out its attitude to food and size.

What we can do about the amount we eat is to be friendly and loving towards ourselves with regard to any imbalance we do feel is there.

Remember the simple statements:

> Moderate diet means pleasant, sweet food,
> leaving free one fourth of the stomach
> > Patanjali *Hatha Yoga Pradipika*

and

> Remember, food is not an enemy
> Portugues and Vedral *Hard Bodies Express Workout*

These are two good starting points.

Take time to discuss with your partner how you feel about food and eating, and any changes you would like to make.

Exercise

The extraordinary obsession with exercise in the 1980s has given way to a kind of anomie in the 1990s. Where, to generalize, people perhaps believed that they could transform themselves by dieting in the 1970s, the magic of transformation in the 1980s was projected onto exercise.

Without doubt we all feel better when we eat well and exercise moderately, but there were certain times in the 1980s when exercise seemed in the collective unconscious to be the Holy Grail through which transcendence would be achieved.

And, naturally, we were disappointed. The fad forms of exercise are receding rapidly, and those which survive are the ancient forms which have long-accrued meanings and rationales of their own (yoga, martial arts), and the forms which have an intrinsic expressive or competitive raison d'etre (dance, sport, athletics). However much we exercise, we cannot turn into something we are not.

To choose a good exercise form to support your efforts in personal safety skills development, all you need to remember is to do some exercise rather than none at all, and to choose exercise where you *find* something rather than exercise where you are trying to *lose* something. (Find the fresh air, the strength, the company, the flexibility, the release, rather than losing the weight, the flab, the bulges). No exercise will ever turn you into a different person – the learning point has to be about self-acceptance, and growing self-recognition, or maybe even, one day, self-love. After all:

> Wherever you go, there you are.

In this way, you will be living more fully in your body, and be more able to learn your core technique and practise it, without self-consciousness and difficulty, until it becomes easy and familiar.

Addictions

What is an addiction? Alcohol, nicotine, heroin, cocaine, are addictive and dangerous drugs. Heroin and cocaine are clearly hazardous and have added dangers attached to them because of the illegality and crime surrounding their supply and use. Alcohol and nicotine, are poisons, and paradoxically have added hazards attached to them precisely because they are legal and accessible. We may also suspect that there are less toxic but just as addictive relationships possible with caffeine and sugar, and widen the meaning of 'addictive' to describe compulsive behaviours – 'shopaholic', 'workaholic', and so on.

If you know you are addicted or tend towards an addition to a drug or a behaviour, it is an important fact to recognize as you try to build your safety skills, your determination to survive. Do not hate yourself or fall into a slough of self-loathing: the courageous recognition that this is where you are now is the first step in moving on and changing things. If you feel at real risk from your addiction, contact Alcoholics Anonymous, or Narcotics Anonymous, or if it is a behavioural addiction, consider finding a therapist or counsellor with whom you can discuss it.

Addiction to drugs, legal or not, has an impact on your safety. At a practical level, any mood-changing drug affects both your ability to assess a situation and your physical coordination if you need to react to it. Smoking clogs your lungs up and makes it harder to run fast or to continue a vigorous struggle for more than a few minutes. At a psychological level, anything that you voluntarily do to yourself which makes you ill, out-of-touch with reality, stressed, and out of control, is an expression of a strand of hatred towards yourself or your life. It is very hard to face up to this, because it may be that your addiction is the safety valve which at present is enabling you to cope with things in yourself or your life which are intolerable. If, however, you are interested enough in your own survival to be reading this at all you may be ready at least to work out how to smoke less, how to be thoughtful about when and where you use alcohol, how to look at compulsive behaviours like workaholism or shopaholism, which are actually ways of beating yourself up, and find your way to being kinder to yourself.

Body language

As we considered while learning 'core technique', the *way* in which you move is significant in safety terms. Even if you are tired, or ill, or sad, or very cold, hungry, or oppressed by some other sensation, walk tall, as if you were relaxed and alert. Lengthen the back of your neck, lengthen the distance between your sternum (breast-bone) and your pubic bone, and keep your shoulders and hips as loose as you can. In fact, moving this way will make you feel better in itself.

Walk decisively in the centre of pavement or path rather than to the edge; at night walk in the best light you can (look around at the light sources and be in the clearest light you can), and remind yourself of your core technique knowledge which you can call upon if you need it. By doing these things your body will tend to manage a quiet preparedness and an inner strength, rather than the dangerous alternatives of a victim-like aura, or an aggression-provoking swagger.

Work practices and life practices

Take time to discuss with your partner what your work practices are and how they may influence your own personal safety. Use the following questions as starting points for your discussion:

- How do you travel to and from work? Are there any risk points around that journey?
- With whom do you come into contact at work? Would you identify any of those people as a potential risk to you?
- Where do you work? What is the building like? Do you use a lift? How is the furniture arranged in your workplace? On reflection, would you identify any of those things as posing a risk?
- Do you travel out from your place of work during the day? Do your colleagues know where you are? If you were out longer than expected on a visit or assignment, is there a system for checking your safety?
- Is there anything else about your work and working practices which, on reflection, you feel might pose a risk to you?

When you have talked these questions through with your partner, take time to go through them with regard to his or her work. Then consider whether there are changes you want to make to your own practices or would like to raise as issues for change or development of new policy at work.

You can also think through the assumptions you make about life practices too.

Ask yourself:

- What kind of transport do I prefer to use? What personal safety questions arise on those forms of transport?
- Where am I prepared to walk alone (a) in daylight (b) after dark? Where do I avoid? How do I assess what feels safe and what feels unsafe?
- What are the points of access to my home? Do I lock them up always/sometimes/never?
- On reflection, is there anything else I want to review in my present basic life practices?

Once again, with your partner take time to talk through your reactions to these questions, and then work through your partner's reactions to them.

When you first begin to think about personal safety issues, you may be depressed by a growing sense of being surrounded by risks. Unpleasant though this is, it is a necessary phase to get through. The risks are there, and have always been there, whether you noticed them or not. Noticing the risks is the first step towards doing something active about them.

Relaxed and alert

Increasing your awareness of risks simply means becoming more alert. The level of reaction to look for is to be *relaxed* and *alert*. Being observant of your life practices and work practices will certainly make you more alert.

Two mnemonics are useful to help you quickly gather details about cars and people – the two things you will most likely need to identify in the event of threat or attack.

For cars:
Colour
Registration (even part of it, especially the year-letter)
Identifying features (such as scratches, cracked lights, bent aerials, etc.)
Make
Exterior shape

For people:
Age
Build
Clothing
Distinguishing features (scars, anything unusual in appearance)
Elevation (height)
Face
Gait

Train yourself to notice these features. Start by trying just to note the first three about a few cars or a few of the people you see in the street. Once you can quickly assimilate

Colour
Registration
Identifying features

or

Age

Build
Clothing

add a couple more items until you can complete the list.

With practice you can give an accurate description of someone you have seen only briefly. You can also, for example give a good description of the data that *is* available to you even if the person is wearing a mask.

Jan, a rape survivor remembered the car mnemonic. She remembered that the car was a particular colour, a particular year-registration, and a particular make. She also noticed that her attacker had a strong Cardiff accent. A computer search turned up 12 cars of that registration, colour and make in Cardiff. The police knocked on only half a dozen of those doors before apprehending her attacker.

Intuition, self-worth, and self-blame

Intuition is a great friend in your development of personal safety skills: it is an ability we need to recognize to value, and to cultivate. Almost every person who has spoken, written, and shared about the experience of being attacked, says that they had an uneasy feeling just prior to the attack which they overrode.

This self-censoring is part of our training to be rational, objective, and intellect-driven. Analytical thinking has of course freed us from many destructive superstitions and demons, but it may sometimes exile us from insights that are helpful and protective. Begin to tune-in to your intuition again. Share with your partner any times when specific intuitions of yours have been correct.

This type of discussion is often light-hearted, consisting mainly of knowing before you pick the phone up who is going to be speaking, or dreaming about an old friend at night and receiving a letter from him or her in the morning's post. Sometimes, though, it is more dramatic:

Paula was happily scrambling along some rocks at the seaside on a sunny day with her child and her boyfriend. Suddenly a chilling premonition of being swept away hit her, and she grabbed the child and ran inland, yelling to her boyfriend to follow. Seconds later a freak wave boiled violently up over rocks where they had been.

At one time I taught yoga preparation for childbirth in a maternity hospital. Every now and again a woman would suddenly ask what to do in the case of a precipitate delivery – i.e. of the baby being born so unexpectedly and so quickly that the woman or her partner had to deliver it herself. I learned always to take time to go through it carefully because every one of the women who asked, it happened to! Some inner knowledge clearly prompted those women to clarify the information they were going to need.

If you have an uneasy feeling about a person, a place, or a situation, learn to listen to that feeling. Do not worry about 'being paranoid'. Of course it takes some time to sift through the signals you need to listen to and those which are hypersensitivity due to just beginning on this track of using intuition. Nevertheless, you will in time, get on the wavelength of intuitions that 'ring true'. All your skills of observation, empathy, assessing moods and atmospheres, come in to help you here.

If you start to feel at risk, even in a familiar place, or even with a familiar person, take your feeling seriously and get out of the situation if you can, raise your preparedness to defend yourself if you cannot. Do not let self-censoring of intuition lead you into an attack that could have been avoided.

Feeling positive about your own intuitive abilities is an important part of developing a sense of self-worth. It is a way of stopping saying to yourself 'I'm probably being stupid', and saying instead to yourself 'I'm probably being wise'.

Acres of print and thousands of hours in millions of lives have been devoted in the last decade or two to enabling those of us who are repressed, confused, and battered by post-war chaotic culture, to feel better about ourselves. 'Personal growth' is an industry in its own right. The way which is right for you is the one which works for you, and makes you feel good about yourself, whatever it may be. It could be professional success, consciousness raising, travelling, fitness, loving, or separateness: nothing works permanently or perfectly, everyone has to cope with regular visits from their old friend, self-doubt. We just have to wrestle with it, as assiduously as we would with a physical attacker. Jnana yoga is the yoga of the intellect. Vivekenanda writes about it:

Our first duty is not to hate ourselves: because to advance we must have faith first in ourselves and then in God.

Vivekenanda *Jnana Yoga*

Self-blame is what happens when we temporarily lose that wrestling match. Linked with physical assault it is the poor sad confused child within each of us which starts to say: 'I caused that attack by being in that place, wearing those clothes, being stupid, ignoring my intuition, not learning my self-defence techniques properly'. You did not, ever. If you feel this way, try to find the warm loving adult within yourself, and get it to put its arms around that stricken child and to tell it: 'You did not cause yourself to be attacked ever, ever, ever. It is not your responsibility'. If you are so hurt that you cannot find that adult voice within yourself, do not hesitate to seek another warm and loving adult to do it for you.

Owning our own violence

The potential for violence is there within all of us. It is not an easy part of our own selves to accept, but acknowledging it is part of being clear that we intend to resist and fight back if necessary if attacked. It is part of seeing that violence is not an 'other' thing that exists only in football hooligans or psychopaths, but that it is a behaviour that any human being is capable of. What matters is what you do with it.

You may recognize your own actual or potential violence in horrifying moments when you lash out or almost lash out at misbehaving children, or hit or almost hit or throw something at a partner whose behaviour is driving you to despair, or feel your temper snap at an inconsiderate motorist or a leering passerby. You have probably learned to contain that first-strike violence in yourself, but you need to look-out for any tendency to turn the violence in on yourself, by anything from actual self-mutilation, to self-damage through alcohol or drug abuse, distorted eating behaviour, or any other self-destructive patterns.

But what are we to do with our anger and despair? Our culture gives us little clue, and we may watch with envy TV pictures of women and men of other cultures wailing, keening, breast-beating, flooding out their grief about personal and political catastrophe. Particularly in the UK, ironic diffidence is expected at all times and allowing even a flow of tears is a major breakthrough. The chief discharge of anger and despair we can allow ourselves is the sublimation model – working hard, training hard, trying hard. Maybe there is time as we run up to the new century, to find other, non-destructive ways of expressing those feelings which almost everybody has at some time.

The violence that a potential attacker, whether it is a stranger or a known person, might use on you, is that same stuff, is that potential inner violence which he or she has failed to contain. You may feel some empathy for the desperation; compassion, even, knowing that nobody would attempt to damage you if he/she was not extremely deeply damaged him-/herself. But you can still be clear in your right and your choice to use force to defend your own body if it is necessary to do so. As we have seen, your body is a fragile enough vehicle for your spirit on this earth, and it is the only one you have. You have the right to protect it.

Loving strength

One last point on attitude follows. Try this visualization; run it through your mind as though it was a film:

> You are walking along a familiar street, the day is ordinary, the sun is shining. You walk round a corner. Suddenly someone attacks you.

Now stop to reflect how you feel. Notice the type of attack you have imagined. Notice the energies and techniques you feel are available to you. Now run this different film:

> You are walking along a familiar street, the day is ordinary, the sun is shining. You walk round a corner. Suddenly, you see somebody you love being attacked.

Once again, reflect on how you feel. Notice the type of attack you have imagined, and what energies and techniques are available to you.

Many people find that when they imagine the first scenario their energies are confused, but that in the second one they feel a surge of energy and determination which allows them to intervene instantly and powerfully.

The question we need to pose to ourselves is that if those energies and that determination are available when a loved one is at risk, could it not also be made available if we are at risk ourselves? Can we learn to love ourselves as much as we love our children, our friends, our partners, our relatives?

If we can, then the huge access to energy and determination we can find is indeed a loving strength which can empower our ability to stay safe.

4

Conclusion

The plan

If you have read, worked with, reacted to the material in this book you have probably experienced all sorts of things: rage, terror, new-found power and strength, maybe inner peace, maybe small or large changes in choices and life paths.

Finally, take some time discussing with your supportive partner, or on your own to formulate in your own mind anything you want to make part of your own plan for staying safe. Do you intend to develop:

- Your fitness?
- Your relationship with food?
- The way you dress?
- Expertise in core technique?
- Life practices?
- Work practices?
- Awareness of addictions?
- Thinking about your own value?

or anything else that has come into your mind as a result of reading and working with these concepts? Note your intentions down as your commitment to yourself. Look at them again after six weeks, six months, and one year. Adapt and change them as you need to as time goes on, and notice and celebrate changes that you wanted to make and have succeeded in doing.

Share with women and men around you the way you feel about safety, power, and the way the world works. At the broadest level, the vision has to be to make every human being aware of the fragility of their body – the muscle, bone, gut and sinew – with which we have to travel and which can, when you start to look at it, be broken and destroyed, so easily. Once anyone is truly aware of his or her fragility, and recognizes that same fragility in everybody else, then the desire that arises is to protect and nurture, and not to damage and destroy either the human body in which *you* live, *or* anybody else's.

Proper body awareness is a wide issue for educationalists, parents, friends and loving humans anywhere. Until that body awareness is there, and while our cities and our rural areas remain dangerous places, while our culture maltreats people so badly that they will seek to relieve their own anguish by preying on others, our responsibility to ourselves has to be to find our own strength, power, and determination to look after ourselves as positively as we can.

Afterword

The 'Heart Sutra'

The word *sutra* means 'stitch' or 'thread' – it is the same root-word as 'suture'. Many Buddhist scriptures are described as *sutras* – they are threads or stitches of thought or insight that need to be woven together to make a full understanding.

I hope this has been a robust and practical book which gives real techniques for the real world which will help to keep you alive.

However, I want to come full circle and leave the last word of the book to the equally important spiritual side of dealing with fear. Equip yourself with the practical knowledge and also take care of your soul. Here you will see Katagiri describing true fearlessness, not as an arrogant state but as a quiet acceptance of the balance of risk and strength and a steady persistence in honesty and self-knowledge.

It was in the mountains and no one was living there. I would hear sounds and it would scare me, but I would tell myself that it was all right and not to worry, nothing would happen. But still I felt as though somebody were following me. . . . Finally I chanted 'Heart Sutra' and I felt good; but immediately when I saw a rabbit . . . I jumped. So the 'Heart Sutra' didn't work. In a sense it was good. I don't mean you should ignore 'Heart Sutra'; temporarily it was nice. But don't expect anything when you chant the 'Heart Sutra'. Just chant the 'Heart Sutra', that is enough . . . it penetrates us, and finally, very naturally, where ever we walk, we don't feel fear.

Dairin Katagiri *Returning to Silence*

Appendix

All-purpose warm-up

When you decide to work on physical core techniques, warm up first:

1. Stand your feet hip-distance apart, and lift up tall out of the pelvis. Relax your shoulders, lift the crown of your head. Rotate your head slowly, three times in one direction, three times in the other. Breathe steadily.
2. Roll your shoulders in slow circles, six times forwards, six times backwards, then shake your arms and hands.

Figure 22

3. Bend your knees a little and put your hands on your hips. Rotate your hips in large slow circles, six times one way, six times the other way.

4. Stretch out to the side in yoga triangle pose (see Figure 21) first one way, and then the other.

5. Sit on the floor, sitting tall, well up out of your hips; the crown of your head lifted and shoulders relaxed. Stretch forwards along your legs to free up your back and hamstrings. Keep the front of your body long. Hold for a few seconds breathing normally. Then sit up.

6. Bring the soles of your feet together and flop your knees out to the sides. Feel the opening in the hips. Remain for a few seconds, breathing normally, then bring your knees up and stretch your legs out.

7. Lie on your tummy on the floor, with your hands placed on the floor at shoulder level. On a breath out, lift the upper body slowly up off the floor like a cobra rising. Use body strength first of all, hand and arm strength last. Keep your shoulders relaxed; your face soft. Remain for a few seconds, breathing normally then flow back down onto the floor again. Now push up onto all-fours and sit back on your heels, leaving your arms and hands extended in front. Feel your lower back release.

8. Do this simple sitting twist known as the *baddha konasana*, first one way and then the other (see Figure 23).

These basic stretches will prepare your body for movement.

Figure 23

Further Reading

Sylvia Brinton Pevera, *Descent to the Goddess*, Inner City Books 1981

Susan Brownmiller, *Against Our Will: Men, Women, and Rape*, Simon and Schuster 1975

Caignon and Groves, eds, *Her Wits About Her: Self-Defence Success Stories by Women*, Women's Press 1987

Ann Jones, *Women Who Kill*, Victor Gollancz 1991

Ritchie McMullan, *Male Rape*, Gay Men's Press 1991

C. W. Nicol, *Moving Zen: Karate as a Way to Gentleness*, Paul Crompton 1981

Paddy O'Brien, *An Introduction to Tae Kwon Do*, Optima 1991

Howard Reid, *The Way of Harmony: A Guide to the Soft Martial Arts*, Unwin Paperbacks 1988

Stozzi and Heckler, eds, *Aikido and the New Warrior*, North Atlantic Books 1985

André van Lysbeth, *Pranayama*, Unwin Hyman 1979

Naomi Wolf, *The Beauty Myth*, Vintage 1990

Useful Addresses

Rape Crisis Line:
Regional centres nationwide: number in telephone directory
Survivors Helpline for male survivors of sexual assault:
071-833 3737, 7–10 p.m. Tuesday & Thursday
Samaritans:
24 hour crisis line: local number in telephone directory
Martial Arts Commission:
Information on classes nationwide: 15–16, Deptford Broadway,
   London SE8 4PA

Choosing a Class

Attending class in a classical martial art will improve your awareness and skill in every way. Choose the style to which you feel
personally drawn, and choose a class which has a calm, controlled
and concentrated feel to it, and a sense of mutual respect and trust
between students and instructor, and among students themselves.

Self-defence classes vary enormously in content and quality.
Look, again, for a class with a calm, controlled atmosphere, a
competent and accurate instructor and a structured approach, and
emphasize the techniques which feel most powerful to you.

Index